Praise for

DAY TRIPS® FROM PHOENIX, TUCSON, AND FLAGSTAFF

"The introduction is practically worth the price of the book with its vital information on when to travel where in Arizona. Thirty-five day trips follow and special directories of 'festivals and celebrations' and the 'great outdoors' complete the picture."
—Family Travel Times

"A calendar of seasonal festivals and celebrations is appended along with lists of national parks, Indian reservations, and tourism associations. A valuable adjunct to more general travel books on the Southwest."
—ALA Booklist

"Presents a diversity of explorations including Indian ruins, ghost towns, lost mines and artist colonies."
—The *Los Angeles Times*

"The descriptions for each trip give clear instructions and basic information about what you will see. Intended for the newcomer and tourist, not the longtime resident."
—Books of the Southwest magazine

"The trips are planned within a convenient drive from the cities, though there are 'worth little more time' sections for not-to-be-missed attractions."
—The (Chicago) *Star*

SHIFRA STEIN'S
DAY TRIPS®
FROM
GREATER PHOENIX, TUCSON and FLAGSTAFF

WRITTEN BY PAM HAIT

EDITED BY SHIFRA STEIN

CHESTER, CONNECTICUT

Library of Congress Cataloging-in-Publication Data

Hait, Pam.
   Shifra Stein's Day Trips® from Greater Phoenix, Tucson, and Flagstaff.

   (Shifra Stein's Day trips)
   Includes index.

   1. Arizona — Description and travel — 1981 — Tours.
2. Phoenix Region (Ariz.) — Description and travel — Tours.
3. Tucson Region (Ariz.) — Description and travel — Tours.
4. Flagstaff Region (Ariz.) — Description and travel — Tours.
I. Stein, Shifra. II. Title. III. Series.

F809.3.H35 1986   917.91'0453   85-71255
ISBN 0-88742-056-7

Section on Flash Floods, Desert Survival, The Climate of Arizona, Heat Wave Safety Rules reprinted from The 1984 KOY Almanac by Gary Edens with permission of Fast & McMillan Publishers, Inc.

Maps by Jim Davenport
Cover design by Kenn Compton
Typography by RJ Publishing, Charlotte, NC
Printed in the United States of America

CONTENTS

Preface: Arizona Travel Tips
Welcome to the Valley of the Sun

Day Trips from Phoenix, 9

N O R T H   F R O M   P H O E N I X

N O R T H E A S T   F R O M   P H O E N I X

E   A   S   T   F   R   O   M   P   H   O   E   N   I   X

SOUTHEAST FROM PHOENIX

SOUTHWEST FROM PHOENIX

WEST FROM PHOENIX

NORTHWEST FROM PHOENIX

Day Trips from Tucson, 77

Day Trips from Flagstaff, 127

FESTIVALS AND CELEBRATIONS

PREFACE
Arizona Travel Tips

Arizona. The name sings with romance. This is the landscape celebrated in Western films where rugged cowboys still ride a vast, rolling range. This is a countryside blessed with sunsets that burst upon the horizon spilling apricot and purple hues as far as you can see. This is a land of immense physical size and unparalleled variety. Mountains and desert, cities and wilderness — Arizona has all of them.

While directions are as clear and exact as possible, you should refer to an Arizona road map as you travel. Write to the Arizona Office of Tourism, 1480 East Bethany Home Rd., Phoenix, AZ. 85014, or call (602) 255-3618 to request a map. You also may write or call the communities or regional tourism information offices of the specific areas you plan to visit and ask for city maps. Read these and refer to them as you travel. Always note the scale of the map. If you are accustomed to eastern maps, you're in for a shock. With 113,909 square miles of land, Arizona is one of the largest states in the nation. One inch on the state road map equals approximately 16 miles!

In addition to its sheer physical size, Arizona is dazzling in its infinite sights, sounds and moods. In a short two-hour trip from the urban centers of Phoenix, Tucson or Flagstaff, you can drive from the floor of the desert to a rocky red precipice and travel in time from pre-historical to frontier days.

There's variety in the climate, too. Wise travelers will consider both the season and their destinations when they plan day trips in and around the three metropolitan areas. Plan summer trips in the Phoenix area with special caution. Because of its low elevation and irrigated Sonoran desert location, the capital city can sizzle under extremely hot daytime temperatures from late May through mid-September. Getting in and out of a hot car saps the enthusiasm of even the most dedicated tourist. In contrast, the fall, winter and early months of spring offer warm days and cool evenings which guarantee almost ideal conditions for driving and sightseeing.

Although Tucson and Phoenix have similar desert climates, because Tucson sits at about 1200 feet higher than Phoenix, Tucson's summer temperatures generally are about ten degrees cooler than those in Phoenix. Tucson is less humid as well, making summer sightseeing slightly more comfortable there than in Phoenix. Winter temperatures in both cities, however, are comparable.

On the other hand, the Flagstaff area offers travelers a radically different experience. Perched at an elevation of over a mile high, Flagstaff's climate is similar to that of Michigan or Wisconsin. The cold winters can come complete with deep snows, making winter day trips around Flagstaff risky. However, a delightful climate with warm, sunny days and cool evenings makes Northern Arizona a perfect vacationland during the spring, summer and fall.

Be prepared for some local idiosyncrasies. For instance, if you ask a direction, you'll generally hear, "It's just 20 minutes down the road," or "That's only a couple of hours away." Arizonans measure distances in time more frequently than in miles. And they think nothing of driving two hours to a destination — that's hardly even a jaunt — which is why many of the day trips included in this book stretch the two-hour getaway time to three hours or sometimes more.

Once you venture even a few miles outside any of the three major cities, you'll often encounter open, empty country. This is a treat for people who love the wild, untamed outdoors, but it can pose challenges for those who prefer urban conveniences. One delightful way to handle the great distances when planning day trips is to carry a picnic lunch. Frequently you will find good restaurants few and far between, so if you don't pack a lunch, you may go hungry. With your picnic handy, you can eat at any of the scenic roadside rest stops. You bring the food; the state provides the ambience with shaded ramadas and sweeping vistas.

Heed road signs at *all* times of the year. If you see a warning: "Not recommended for sedan travel," believe it! Arizona roads can be rugged and extremely rough on automobiles. When driving through country marked "open range," be alert. Although a rare occurrence, you could encounter loose cows, sheep or other livestock wandering across the road. Obey both flash flood warnings and dust storm warnings. That dry wash may appear harmless, but a wash can quickly turn into a deadly torrent if a sudden rainstorm occurs. Never take foolish chances trying to cross flooded areas. Specific directions for dealing with flash floods are included in the back of this book.

Safe driving in the desert demands that travelers take certain precautions. Arid lands can be unforgiving especially during the hot summer months. Always carry water in your car for emergencies. You may need it for drinking or cooling an overheated engine. If you travel during the heat of the summer, try to accomplish most of your driving during the early morning hours or after the sun sets. Always tell someone where you are going and when you expect to return. If you are overdue, somebody will know when to start worrying and can alert the authorities. If you have car problems, stay with your vehicle. Don't wander off for help; let help find you. Refer to the back of the book for desert survival tips.

Finally, don't hike into the wilderness alone. Even experienced hikers get lost.

You can take every day trip and hike described in this book without ever running into any of the emergency situations mentioned above. Arizona is **not** hazardous to your health. If you treat this unique and often untamed landscape with the respect it deserves, however, you can have safe and exhilarating experiences. What's more, you will be free to appreciate its magnificence and learn to love it as I do.

Pam Hait

USING THIS BOOK

In most cases, hours were omitted because they are subject to frequent changes. Instead, phone numbers are listed for obtaining up-to-date information.

Restaurant prices are designated as $$$ (Expensive: $15 and over); $$ (Moderate: $5 to $15); $ (Inexpensive: $5 and under).

You will also find the symbol □ to denote that credit cards are accepted.

Day Trips
From Phoenix

Welcome to Phoenix, capital city of the state of Arizona and hub of "The Valley of the Sun." The valley is surrounded by mountain ranges, clear cool lakes, and more five-star resorts than any metropolitan area in the country — a veritable paradise for tourists. Because visitors have such a choice of accommodations, it is suggested that you write to the Arizona Hotel & Motel Association, 3003 North Central Ave., 61204, Phoenix, AZ 85012, and request a brochure describing the hotels, motels, dude ranches and cabins in the state. Or you may call (602) 264-6081 for information.

With Phoenix as your starting point, you'll be amazed to discover how much variety awaits you even in a two-hour drive. Some easy day trips can take you to urban areas, such as Scottsdale, Mesa, Tempe or even Tucson. On other trips, you can climb quickly from the desert floor to mountainous pine forests, or you can enter a time warp that takes you back to pioneer and ancient Indian eras.

Ideally, visitors to Arizona should plan to spend some vacation time in Phoenix, Tucson and Flagstaff, taking day trips from each. In this way, you'll get a true flavor of the state. A second plan could include Phoenix as your hub, because it is centrally located and is the largest metropolitan area in the state. As you journey around the Phoenix environs, you'll soon discover that many of the Phoenix-based trips easily fall within the two-hour limitation. In some cases, you'll need to drive longer than two hours; however, each trip is worth it.

If you use Flagstaff as your starting point for several of the Phoenix-based day trips, you can cut your travel time by an hour or even more.

The vast majority of tourists, however, start their day trips from the Phoenix metropolitan area, rather than from the smaller northern Arizona community of Flagstaff.

As you read along, you'll note that many of the itineraries described can be done as overnight instead of a single day's journey. If you have the time, it's always nice to stay over in a destination town. That way you can spend more hours seeing the sights and exploring the area, proportionately less time on the road.

One last piece of advice. As you peruse the Phoenix section of this book, you'll read about sights to see, canyons to explore, side roads to wander, shops not to miss and special trips to take. In your enthusiasm to do it all, don't overload yourself. This is especially true when traveling during the summer, because the high desert temperatures can be extremely tiring. If you decide to visit a museum or Indian ruin, allow enough time to study the exhibits or soak up the atmosphere of a few selected attractions rather than rushing from point to point. The essential Arizona experience is a casual, laid-back lifestyle. Whether sitting at a sidewalk cafe in Scottsdale or standing silently before Montezuma Castle, don't push yourself to cover too much too fast.

For brochures, maps and specific information on the fascinating Phoenix metropolitan area, contact the Phoenix & Valley of The Sun Convention & Visitors Bureau, 4455 E. Camelback Rd., Suite 146, Phoenix, AZ 85018, or call (602) 254-6500.

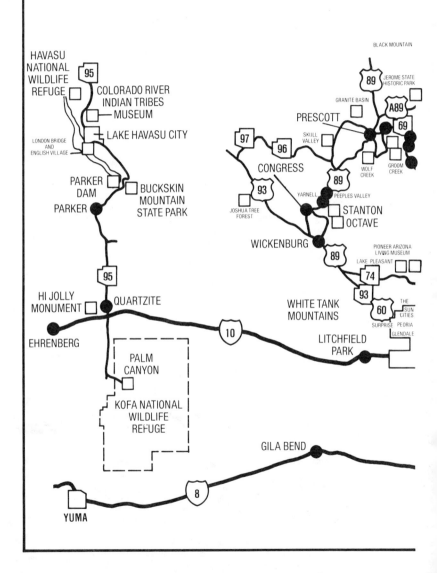

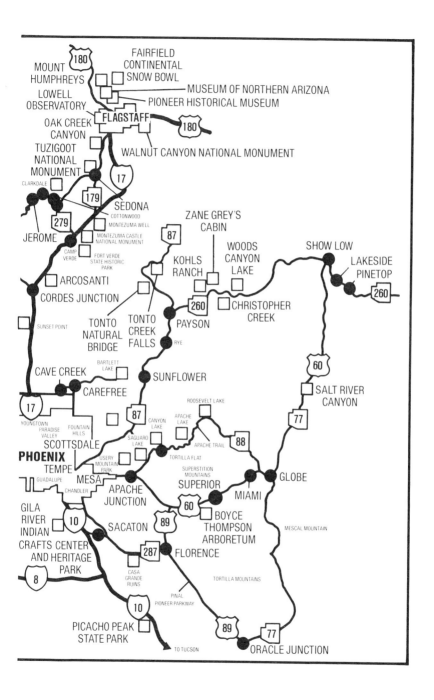

Day Trip 1

PRESCOTT
YARNELL-PEEPLES VALLEY

PRESCOTT

This trip covers some of the same territory found in Day Trip 2, North From Phoenix. However, in this itinerary, Prescott is the primary destination. A pine-studded jewel of a town two hours north of Phoenix, and once the capital of the Territory of Arizona, it is the seat of Yavapai County. It's famous for its Victorian-style homes, Fourth of July celebrations and temperate climate. Since there are so many scenic drives in the Prescott area, you may want to spend the entire day there.

Prescott offers cool summer days and moderate winter days, so it's always safe to take a sweater or lightweight jacket with you. If possible, visit during any of the festivals and celebrations which occur during every month of the year. Obtain details from the Prescott Chamber of Commerce at 117 W. Goodwin St. 86301, or call (602) 445-2000.

To reach Prescott, follow I-17 north to Cordes Junction. Take A-69 northwest and meander past the small towns of Mayer, Humbolt, Dewey and Prescott Valley. The largest of these communities is Mayer, which is located in the foothills of the Bradshaw Mountains. Founded in 1881 by Joseph Mayer, it began as a store, saloon, and Wells Fargo Stage station. Mayer was a stop along the stage line between Phoenix and Prescott. Today, it continues the tradition as a stop along A-69 for motorists.

Enter Prescott on A-69 west until it meets Gurley Street. Travel left on Gurley past Marina Street and you're in the heart of town. Park anywhere between Cortez and Montezuma streets for your tour of this historic area.

As you gaze at the gingerbread homes and tall brick buildings, you may think that Prescott is an unlikely Arizona town. Remember that the desert, with its low-slung adobe structures, is only one Arizona image. In the more northern parts of the state, two-story brick and wood buildings are just as appropriately an "Arizona" style.

Here territorial Arizona springs to life. Prescott flourished when the area was a wild and untamed place. As military personnel and miners moved in, no doubt they were anxious to make it seem like home, so they built what they knew: "back-East" buildings, proper brick and two-story structures reminiscent of Ohio or Pennsylvania.

The first capital of the Arizona Territory, Prescott ultimately lost its bid to become the permanent state capital. The honor went to Phoenix instead. Still, much Arizona history was made here and fortunately, for visitors, remains well preserved.

WHERE TO GO

Courthouse Plaza. This is the area bounded by Cortez and Montezuma, Gurley and Goodwin streets. It's a real town square that functions much as it did during territorial times. During festivals, the grassy square is lined with booths, and people sprawl on the lawns. In more quiet times, you can soak up the serenity that the solid courthouse building exudes. After you've enjoyed the courthouse, wander the streets to explore the galleries and stores. Although Prescott is a tourist mecca, it has resisted ticky-tacky tourist shops. You'll find a real community here, not cardboard storefront images.

Sharlot Hall Museum. 415 W. Gurley St. This museum is actually a number of separate buildings grouped together to give visitors a living panorama of Southwestern history. Spanning the years from the founding of Prescott in 1864 to the present, the buildings appear to be in architectural sequence. You can tour the Governor's Mansion which was built on this site in 1864 from local ponderosa pine. Several territorial officials, including Governor John Goodwin, lived in this mansion.

The John C. Fremont House. Built in 1875, it is constructed of wood and reflects the rapid growth Prescott experienced during its first ten years. Fremont, known as "the Pathfinder," served as the fifth territorial governor of Arizona from 1878 to 1881.

Arizona became a state February 14, 1912. The William C. Bashford House represents the type of architecture common to the area during the two decades before statehood. Complete with a solarium, this house was built in another location and moved to the museum grounds in 1974.

The **Sharlot Hall** building, completed in 1934, is the primary exhibit hall and includes the Museum Shop and display rooms for pre-Columbian artifacts, historic Southwestern items, and old photographs. These pictures capture the essence of what it was like for white and red men to live in this territory over 100 years ago. This exhibit is all the more remarkable when you realize that Indians feared — and some still do fear — the camera, believing that it takes away a man's soul.

Who was Sharlot Hall that an entire enclave of a museum is devoted to her? She was an outstanding woman — a writer, poet, collector of Arizona artifacts and territorial historian — who moved to Arizona from Kansas in 1882. She remained fascinated with Arizona until her death in 1943.

As you stroll along the sidewalks which circle and connect the museum's major buildings, you can visit other memorials and exhibits, including the Blacksmith Shop, one of the town's first boarding houses, which the frontiersmen called "Fort Misery;" a replica of Prescott's first public school; and the Pioneer Herb and Memorial Rose garden. Donation requested. Open daily. (602) 445-3122.

Whiskey Row. Montezuma Street between Goodwin and Aubrey Streets. This is Prescott's famous "wicked" street. The name says it all. Everyone needs to walk up Whiskey Row, even if they aren't thirsty. In the old days, it was almost one long bar — for saloons lined the entire street. Today, it's more sedate except, during festivals and celebrations. Then the Old West springs to life again as cowboys belly up to the crowded bars.

Prescott Historical and Gold Panning Tours. Prescott and the Bradshaw Mountains. Several years ago Melissa Ruffner, dressed in authentic period costumes, began giving tours of Prescott's Victorian homes. Since then, she and her partner have expanded their business. In addition to walking tours of the four-block historical district, they take groups to working gold claims in the Bradshaw Mountains.

Call ahead to find out more about this trip. You'll need good walking shoes, a sack lunch and, if you care about your manicure, gloves. Ms. Ruffner also puts together specialty tours of Prescott, which can cover anything from how the frontier settlers used solar energy to the area's early religious or ethnic populations. Fee. Contact Melissa Ruffner, (602) 445-4567.

SCENIC DRIVES

Granite Dells. Drive east on Gurley Street, and north on US-89 for about four miles. Just north of Prescott, nature has carved a sculpture garden of ancient rock formations. As you approach, you'll notice that the rocks appear to have human or animal forms. That's Mother Nature, the artist, at work. Centuries of wind, rain, snow and sun worked on this granite cliff to form these eerie figures. Formerly known as the "Point of Rocks," the Granite Dells is set off by Watson Lake, a clear blue pool which contrasts vividly with the subtle colors of the smooth, round boulders.

Granite Mountain and Granite Basin. This trip will take about 20 minutes each way. Drive west on Gurley Street to Grove Avenue. Turn right on Grove and continue out Miller Valley Road. Bear left at the junction of Iron Springs and Willow Creek roads onto Iron Springs and continue to the Prescott National Forest sign on the right side of the road. Turn right and continue to Granite Basin Recreation site, a unique geological and historical wilderness area. Long before Congress declared the Granite Mountain Trail a national recreation area in 1979, hikers and rock climbers were well acquainted with its spectacular scenery. If you are in good shape and dressed for outdoor action, you can hike to the overlook. Otherwise, walk the trails and marvel at the sheer, smooth cliffs.

Lynx Lake. Fifty-five acres of lake just 15 minutes away! Follow A-69 east for four miles to Walker Road. Turn right for approximately three miles. Lynx Lake, which is fed by nearby Lynx Creek, has a rich history. Gold was discovered at the creek during territorial days giving frontiersmen and women even more reason to make the trip to Prescott. Fishing is good year-round, and during the summer, you can rent a boat from the lakefront concession. Take your sweetheart on a moonlight cruise across the smooth, clear waters.

Senator Highway Drive. This is an hour's round-trip but well worth it, especially if you like to relive history. Drive east on Gurley Street to South Mt. Vernon/Senator Highway. Along the way, you'll pass by Groom Creek, which was a Mormon settlement. Turn right on South Mt. Vernon Senator Highway and head south to Wolf Creek picnic grounds. If you are so inclined, head for either Wolf Creek or Lower Wolf Creek campgrounds where you can hike, picnic or if you trailer them in with you, do some four-wheeling on all-terrain vehicles (ATC's). Continue following this road to the right as it goes down the pine-studded mountain to the Indian Creek picnic grounds. Join US-89 six miles from Prescott. Turn right and continue back to town. This used to be an old stage route connecting Prescott with Crown Point. As you make this drive, you can imagine how the pioneers felt as they bounced along on rutted roads shaded by these tall ponderosas.

Skyline Drive (also called Thumb Butte Loop). Plan on 45 minutes to cover this truly spectacular drive. Head south on Montezuma Street (US-89) to Copper Basin Road. Turn right on Copper Basin Road, make a circle and return to Thumb Butte Road. Along the way you will see the Sierra Prieta Mountain range which overlooks Skull Valley. As you approach Thumb Butte, you'll have a panoramic view of the San Francisco Peaks. These mountains are sacred to the Hopis who believe that these peaks are home to their Kachina gods. During this drive, you'll ascend some 1500 to 1700 vertical feet. If you think this is a steep drive, imagine what it's like to *run* up this road. The Whiskey Row Marathon Society uses it as its course.

Along the way, you'll see a number of places to pull off to drink in the views. Be sure to do so when you see a viewpoint for Skull Valley. The name, Skull Valley, came from a group of calvarymen who discovered mounds of sun-bleached skulls there in 1884. Later it was decided that these were the skulls of Apache and Maricopa Indians who clashed over stolen horses.

If you're dressed properly and not bothered by the altitude, take advantage of the hiking trails. These are well marked. A 2.3-mile trail leads to Thumb Butte. It begins easily. For almost a mile you can stroll along shaded ponderosa pines and three kinds of oak trees. Gradually, the vegetation changes...the pines recede and junipers, prickly pears, pinyons and other scrub vegetation gain on you as the trail approaches the exposed ridge. You'll come to a junction at 1.1 miles. To the left, the trail rises to the base of the butte. This climb involves 200 feet of steep cliff and is not recommended for non-climbers. Instead, hikers should follow the right fork and continue about 150 yards to a vista point. When you reach it, you'll understand why you've made this trip.

Short trails also lead to Mount St. Francis and West Spruce Mountain. When you're tired and hiked out, head back to your car and continue into Prescott on West Gurley Street.

WHERE TO EAT

Murphy's. 201 N. Cortez St. In this general store setting, you can munch on mesquite-broiled seafood or chow down on a variety of entrees, including excellent prime rib. $$; □. (602) 445-4044.

Prescott Mining Company. 155 Plaza Dr. Great for fresh fish, prime rib and steaks. The outdoor patio is a standout. Eat amidst a sylvan setting of flowers and trees (and ignore the new condos in the distance). $$; □. (602) 445-1991.

The Palace Hotel and Restaurant. 116 S. Montezuma St. Located on Whiskey Row, this historic building is jammed with photographs and fascinating memorabilia. It's worth a visit just to tour the building. Once you're inside and the hungry juices flow, you can order seafood, steaks or poultry. $$; □. (602) 778-6225.

YARNELL and PEEPLES VALLEY

To return most directly to Phoenix, head south on US-89 through Yarnell and Peeples Valley. The road bisects the densely wooded Prescott National Forest and is exceptionally scenic. You'll be looking at the Sierra Prieta Mountains or the Black Mountains named by the Spaniards who explored this part of the state. The latter owe their dark color to their volcanic origin.

Peeples Valley is named for Abraham Peeples, who supposedly gathered between $4000 and $7000 worth of gold nuggets before breakfast one morning when he was walking on Weaver Mountain. Not surprisingly, the area commemorating Peeples' find is called "Rich Hill."

For more scenic beauty, follow A-96 (a back road) west from Prescott as it meanders past Iron Springs and into Skull Valley. The views are as great as the names. Where A-96 intersects with A-97, follow A-97 toward Phoenix for 16 miles to where it joins US 93-89. Follow US 93-89 to Wickenburg, Surprise and Sun City; about 60 miles northwest of Phoenix the route becomes US-60.

Day Trip 2

PIONEER ARIZONA LIVING MUSEUM
CORDES JUNCTION
CAMP VERDE
MONTEZUMA CASTLE NATIONAL MONUMENT
YAVAPAI APACHE VISITOR CENTER
MONTEZUMA HALL
JEROME

PIONEER ARIZONA LIVING MUSEUM

Prepare to move through time from a prehistoric era to the future. The drive begins in rolling desert but climbs into steep mountain terrain in Jerome. You'll begin with endless vistas and, as the mountains close in around you, saguaros give way to scrub and ultimately to sycamores. This landscape is filled with silent memories of the Sinaguas, an ancient Indian tribe who lived here hundreds of years ago. During the late 1800s, this countryside was alive with the ring of picks and shovels and the shouts of prospectors who worked in Rawhide Jimmy Douglas's silver mines.

Although the driving time from Phoenix to Jerome is three hours, this is considered a full-day trip in this land of wide open spaces. Should you choose to hike *and* sightsee, you'll arrive home in the evening tired but happy.

Start off early and take I-17 north toward Camp Verde to the Pioneer Arizona Living Museum. Plan to arrive around 9 a.m. to do this trip easily in a day.

WHERE TO GO

Pioneer Arizona Living Museum. 1879 wedding chapel, Black Canyon Freeway and Pioneer Road. On I-17, twelve miles north of Bell Road, take exit 225 and follow signs to the museum. You'll spend a good hour touring the many authentic and replicated buildings on the grounds of this privately supported museum. Although a restaurant exists here, it's closed Tuesdays. A shaded picnic area is always open. Call ahead for museum hours. Fee. (602) 993-0212.

Sunset Point. Follow the signs back to I-17 north. You may want to stop for a breathtaking view at this unique roadside rest stop, winner of an architectural award for excellence. Along with a sweeping panorama, you'll find a map, clean restrooms and picnic tables.

CORDES JUNCTION

Back on I-17 north, continue to the Cordes Junction exit and Arcosanti, where you can visit a unique construction site.

WHERE TO GO

Arcosanti. I-17 at Cordes Junction, Mayer. Turn right at Cordes Junction Road and left at the stop sign. Follow a dirt road about three miles to Arcosanti — architect Paolo Soleri's vision of the future. Called the boldest experiment in urban living in the country, this energy-efficient town which integrates architecture and ecology has been under construction since 1970.

Soleri coined the word "arcology" to express his vision of a community in which people can live and work in harmony with the environment. In designing this prototype "city" under a single roof, Soleri combines an urban environment with a natural setting all within one structure. Ultimately, Soleri's plan utilizes both above and underground space to concentrate human activity into an energy efficient environment while carefully leaving the vast surrounding acreage natural and undisturbed.

Arcosanti is being built by students and professionals who work and attend seminars on the site. Festivals and performances by visiting artists are scheduled during the year. Daily tours are available. A donation is suggested. (602) 632-7135.

WHERE TO EAT

Arcosanti. The cafe on the site serves breakfast and lunch and features homemade foods prepared without preservatives or additives. A kids' menu is available. The cafe is not fancy, but the food is hearty and healthy. $-$$. □. (602) 632-7135.

CAMP VERDE

As you follow I-17 north, it plunges into a long downgrade which reveals the Verde Valley in all its splendor. If you've not been this way before, pull off at the marked scenic viewpoints and enjoy grand vistas along the way to this historic area.

WHERE TO GO

Fort Verde State Historical Park. Lane Street, Camp Verde. Take the first Camp Verde exit, 285, follow that road into Camp Verde, and turn right onto Lane Street. Visit the 10-acre Fort Verde Historical Park and see where Gen. George Crook accepted the surrender of Apache Chief Chalipun and 300 of his warriors in 1873. Crook left a distinctive mark on Arizona. In addition to his meeting with the Apache chief, Calipun, the general had a rough wagon road cut up and along the Mogollon Rim in 1884 to shorten the distance between Fort Apache and Fort Verde. Even today, that area is referred to as Crook's Trail.

Fort Verde was a major base for General Crook's scouts, soldiers and pack mules during the Indian campaigns of the 1870s. As you walk the dusty street of Officer's Row, you'll return to territoral days and better understand what it was like for the officers and their families who lived at Fort Verde during this period in history.

Tour the officers' quarters overlooking the parade ground, which are furnished in authentic 1880's military style. As you continue walking through the park, you may wonder at the Post Surgeon's spacious accommodations. In those days, patients were treated and surgery performed in the doctor's residence, while the post hospital was used only for quarantine and convalescence. Fee for adults only. Open daily. (602) 567-3649.

MONTEZUMA CASTLE NATIONAL MONUMENT

To travel further back in time, follow Montezuma Castle Road five miles north from Camp Verde to Montezuma Castle National Monument. The ancient five-story Indian dwelling is carved out of a great limestone cliff. Although Indians lived in the valley as early as 600 A.D., it's believed that Sinagua farmers began building this dwelling sometime during the twelfth century A.D. When it was completed about three centuries later, the dwelling contained 19 rooms, many of them suitable for living space.

The name Montezuma Castle is a misnomer. Montezuma, the Aztec King, never slept here. In fact, he was never here at all. When pioneers discovered the cliff dwelling, they mistook it for an ancient Aztec settlement and named it Montezuma Castle. Although the historical inaccuracy was determined later, the name stuck.

Stop at the visitors center first before taking the self-guided tour. Take time to view the hand-fitted stone walls and foot-thick sycamore ceiling beams; then, let your imagination fly.

There is a fee which also covers Montezuma Well. Open daily. (602) 567-3322.

YAVAPAI-APACHE VISITOR CENTER

Yavapai-Apache Visitor Center. Located at the junction of I-17 and Middle Verde Road. This area is rich in Indian and Arizona history. The Yavapai-Apache tribe is noted for its basketry. The visitors center houses a tribal museum and arts and crafts exhibit. Open daily. Free. (602) 567-5276.

MONTEZUMA WELL

Back on I-17 north, continue a few miles to the McGuireville exit. Follow the side road to Montezuma Well, but be ready for a bumpy, rough ride. This limestone sink was formed centuries ago by a collapsed cavern. Springs feed it continuously, and both the Hohokam Indians (who settled the Phoenix area in pre-Columbian times) and the Sinagua used the well for crop irrigation. This area contains a Hohokam pithouse built around 1100 A.D., and Sinaguan dwellings. It's estimated that around 150 to 200 Sinaguans lived here between 1125 A.D. and 1400 A.D. when apparently they were forced out by a drought. The fee covers both Montezuma Castle and Montezuma Well. Open daily. (602) 567-4521.

JEROME

This area is as rich in lore as it was in ore. Although the steep ascent into Jerome is not for the faint of heart, it's an unforgettable "living" ghost town. Jerome boomed in 1876. Gold and silver flowed, and people poured in. Today, all that remains of its former glory teeters on the precipitous slopes of Cleopatra Hill, about 5000 feet above sea level. The twisted, narrow streets, reminiscent of Europe, inspire the most unimaginative photographer, so bring your camera and lots of film.

To get to Jerome from Montezuma Well, backtrack to I-77 South and A-279. From Montezuma Castle, pick up A-279 at I-17 and head northwest for 12 to 15 miles toward Jerome. Just north of Bridgeport, A-279 joins US-89A; follow US-89A into Jerome.

WHERE TO GO

Tuzigoot National Monument. If you are up for more Indian ruins, don't veer west onto US-89A, but continue north on A-279 to see another Sinaguan village. This ancient ruin is located between Cottonwood and Clarkdale and was forgotten until the 1930s when a team of archeologists from the University of Arizona began excavating and exploring it. Their work was amply rewarded. They deducted that the original pueblo was two stories high and had 77 ground-floor rooms. Built between 1125 A.D. and 1400 A.D., this ruin offers yet another intimate view of the ancient people who roamed, hunted and farmed here. The pueblo is situated on a 120-foot high ridge presenting a panoramic view of the Jerome-Clarkdale area. No doubt the Sinaguas stood there, centuries ago, and marveled at the undisturbed view.

Spend some time to walk the trail at Tuzigoot. If you are fascinated by these people, don't leave without visiting the museum. Open daily. Fee. (602) 634-5564.

Jerome State Park. UVX Road. Originally the home of mining pioneer James S. Douglas, the state park features an extensive display of mining equipment. Museum lovers should follow UVX Road to the park where exhibits recounting the story of this once-flourishing copper mining community are displayed. As you browse through the mansion of "Rawhide" Jimmy, as he was known, you'll gain a sense of the personalities, places and technology which forged this period of Arizona history.

You'll need to retrace your steps to US-89A when you leave here. Open daily. Fee. (602) 634-5381.

Main Street. Jerome. US-89A becomes Main Street as it continues into Jerome. Park anywhere and walk around to get a sense of this special community. Now a popular tourist stop, Jerome almost became a ghost town; however, it's safe to assume that the ghosts now have left for quieter spots. Revived during the 1960s when hippies discovered that it was both cheap and charming, today Jerome is a haven for people who eschew the urban scene.

As you walk around, you may want to stop in the shops, galleries and restaurants which flourish in this area. Don't expect any uptown flash. Jerome is long on quaintness and short on commercial appeal. It's worth your time to spend a few minutes in the Jerome Historical Society on the corner of Main and Jerome streets to learn more about the town. You may contact the Jerome Historical Society at P.O. Box 156, Jerome, AZ 86331, or call (602) 634-5477 in advance to request a town map and more information. While you are at the historical society, visit the Mine Museum in the building to see artifacts and exhibits illustrating Jerome's past glory.

Alfredo's Wife. Main Street. If you love whimsical, hand-appliqued clothing, visit "Alfredo's Wife." The designer, known only as Alfredo's Wife (and there really is an Alfredo), has built a devoted clientele who love her signature — a little mouse. The clothing and gift items are all handmade by a cadre of local ladies who stitch the designs. Alfredo's Wife has stores in Scottsdale and Sedona and a workshop in Cottonwood, but this local woman began her business in Jerome, so this is an ideal place to become acquainted with her one-of-a-kind styles.

WHERE TO EAT

The House of Joy. Hull Avenue, one block below Main Street. A converted bordello, with lots of red velvet, gas lamps and an upstairs which once catered to "business," this restaurant offers homemade gourmet food and old-time Jerome atmosphere. Open Saturdays and Sundays only. Dinner. Reservations are required. Call ahead after 9 a.m. Saturdays and Sundays. $$; no cards. (602) 634-5339.

Day Trip 3

SEDONA
OAK CREEK CANYON

SEDONA

This is one of the most popular day trips for visitors and residents alike. Desert dwellers love the lush green of Oak Creek Canyon and one never tires of the Red Rocks or the startling view as the highway plunges into the heart of this magnificent country. Dedicated shoppers enjoy poking around the intriguing boutiques and art galleries in Sedona and the village of Oak Creek. Outdoor buffs have a veritable banquet to choose from — everything from water sports to Indian ruins to hiking, to running or jogging up Schnebley Hill for the more hardy.

Although you can approach Sedona in a couple of ways, I-17 north to A-179 is a popular route. At the junction of A-179 and US-89A, head north on A-179 and continue toward Sedona. The trip is an easy, non-stop, two-hour drive from Phoenix. Along the way, you get a full dose of Sedona's famous Red Rocks, one of the reasons for the town's popularity. Although recently man has made his mark here with condominiums, shopping centers and elegant homes, the Red Rocks still dominate the landscape. At an elevation of 4300 feet, Sedona's weather is usually delightful. Although snow occasionally falls in winter and summer temperatures can peak from warm to hot, the climate generally is ideal. You can easily spend a day (not to mention money) exploring indoors. Sedona offers a full complement of culture and recreation. Outdoor enthusiasts will find plenty to do. The area is rich with campgrounds and Indian ruins. Hatcheries keep the fishing good. Between the glorious apricot-to-peach-to-purple sunsets and the burnished Red Rocks, Sedona is awash with color.

WHERE TO GO

Chapel of the Holy Cross. Heading toward Sedona on A-179, you pass the Village of Oak Creek. Continue on A-179, for approximately five miles. In the distance, on your right, you will see the Chapel of the Holy Cross against the Red Rocks. Turn right on Chapel Road which leads to the church. The road is well marked with three signs announcing the turn off. This is an inspirational and architectural treat. It is open daily to the public free of charge. (602) 282-4069.

Tlaquepaque. Continue north on A-179. As it bends right before crossing Oak Creek, make a sharp left turn. The entrances are immediately on your left. The cobblestone driveways are marked by rustic-looking stone gates which are almost hidden beneath the tall trees.

Tlaquepaque (Ta-la-kee-pahkee) is a shopping center worth your time. Named for a suburb of Guadalajara, Mexico, this is a favorite gathering place for locals and tourists. Indulge yourself in the boutiques featuring everything from superb pottery, elegant glass, clothing, and gifts to art and sculpture. You can also feed your body, as well as your soul, at a number of excellent dining establishments.

This special center features Mexican (albeit made-to-look-old) colonial village ambience. Even if you don't enjoy shopping, you'll like sitting on the stone benches, soaking up the fragrance of the flowers and sounds of the many fountains.

As you walk through Tlaquepaque, notice the bell tower which is a Sedona landmark. Peek inside the tiny chapel near the central plaza. Just as each Spanish and Mexican village has a church, Tlaquepaque has its chapel which holds approximately 20 people and is used for private weddings and other ceremonies. For more information, contact the Tlaquepaque Merchants Association, P.O. Box 1868, Sedona, AZ 86336. (602) 282-4838.

The Red Rocks. There's no better way to see the rocks than in a Pink Jeep. Sedona's famous **Pink Jeep Tours** offer adventure for everyone who is daring enough to ride off the road and up the hills and over the creeks to gain this special view of the majestic Sedona landscape. You may call ahead to reserve space on one of the seven jeeps. The tour guide meets you at the Canyon Portal Motel on US-89A. Take anywhere from a one-hour to a three-hour tour, or sign up for a rollicking all-day trip. This excursion is recommended for all ages, but be prepared for some wild driving and even wilder views. For more information about times and prices, write Pink Jeep Tour, P. O. Box 1447, Sedona, AZ 86336. Fee. (602) 282-5000.

Honanki. Inquiring minds will jump at the chance to follow Warren Cremer, an adventurous guide, who will escort you on an archeological expedition. Cremer, an archeologist and anthropologist, conducts back-country tours by jeep to an unexcavated, unreconstructed cliff dwelling which you'll explore, room by room. As you do, you'll share Cremer's knowldege, awe and wonder. Reserve a two and a half hour expedition, a 35-minute helicopter archeological overview, or follow Cremer on his extended three-hour tour, which includes an extra treat. Cremer packs a gourmet picnic lunch for his guests. Write to Warren Cremer, Time Expeditions, P. O. Box 2936, Sedona AZ 86336, or phone (602) 282-2137.

WHERE TO EAT

L'Auberge de Sedona. 301 Little Lane, Sedona. On US-89A, one block north of AZ-179. This country inn is the newest and most posh establishment in Sedona. You can rent a cabin or simply come for breakfast, lunch or a five-course, fixed-price dinner. Call for reservations. $$-$$$; □. (602) 282-1661.

The Oak Creek Owl. AZ-179, or Box 553, Sedona, AZ 86336. This is a long-time Sedona landmark known for its views, ambience and good food. The cozy restaurant features lunch and dinner in an elegant setting which overlooks Oak Creek. $$; □. (602) 282-3532.

Renees. Tlaquepaque. This authentic French restaurant features great french bread and superb cuisine. The house specialty is an excellent rack of lamb. Don't be turned away by the French ambience. Inside, you'll find elegantly casual surroundings. You can come as you are, dressed for sightseeing. $$; □. (602) 282-9225.

OAK CREEK CANYON

Oak Creek Canyon is just north of Sedona on US 89-A. Don't see one without seeing the other. Oak Creek glimmers in autumn, sparkles cool and clear in summer, and occasionally is tinged with winter snow. The drive through Oak Creek Canyon is steep enough to satisfy a roller-coaster lover, but once on the canyon floor, you may park your car and walk around the area.

For many sightseers, the drive through Oak Creek Canyon is experience enough. More ambitious types should take a casual stroll through the wooded area along the creek. Serious hikers may prefer more rugged challenges, so if you don't mind getting wet (you'll need to wade across the creek), there are more rigorous routes described in several books on outdoor Arizona available at local bookstores.

Day Trip 4

FLAGSTAFF

FLAGSTAFF

Often called "the city of seven wonders," Flagstaff is approximately three hours north of Phoenix, an easy day trip by Arizona standards. The scenic highway dips through the Verde Valley, climbs over the Mogollon Rim, or "the Rim" as it's better known, and ultimately reaches this 7000-foot-high city. This is a trip of strong natural contrasts: you travel from prickly pears to pines. If you take this drive in winter, you can swim in your heated Phoenix pool in the morning, ski all afternoon in Flagstaff, and return home to Phoenix that night!

Trivia lovers may enjoy knowing that most stories concerning the origin of the name Flagstaff involve some person lopping off branches of a lone pine and running a flag up the pole. Fortunately, someone thought "Flag-staff" had a better ring to it than "Flag-pole." In any event, it is documented that to celebrate the naming, a centennial flag was flown from a tall pine tree on July 4, 1876.

Today, this city is the seat of Coconino County, second largest county in the country and home to Northern Arizona University. The northern hub of the state, Flagstaff is a bustling little city, which is bisected by railroad tracks, surrounded by pines, and dominated by the 12,670-foot Mount Humphreys Peak, the tallest mountain in the state. Surrounded by verdant splendor, the older downtown area is ringed with appealing newer sections featuring reddish wood tones and rustic, ski-lodge motifs. During ski season, Flagstaff's Fairfield Continental Snow Bowl hums with the whoosh of downhill skiers coursing down Mount Humphreys. Throughout the year, the city is home to a hardy breed of students and outdoor types. If you love plaid flannel shirts, this may be your place. With Flagstaff as your jumping-off point, the whole of northern Arizona opens up and a wonderland of day trips opens to you. (Read about these in the section titled DAY TRIPS FROM FLAGSTAFF.) In the meantime, here's a sampling of the sights to see when you visit this hub of northern Arizona.

WHERE TO GO

Lowell Observatory. 1400 W. Mars Hill Rd. Travel west on Santa Fe Avenue; following the street to the end, climb Mars Hill. Dr. Percival Lowell built the wooden, world-famous observatory in 1894. The planet Pluto was discovered here in 1930, and today the observatory continues to be a center of important scientific work. Interesting and informative guided tours are available on weekdays. If you visit during the summer, plan on spending Friday night here when the observatory is open free to the public by ticket only. Write in advance to the Flagstaff Chamber of Commerce, 101 W. Santa Fe Ave., Flagstaff, AZ 86001 or call (602) 774-4505 for reservations. Tickets may be picked up at the Chamber of Commerce during the day. Donation suggested. Call observatory for hours at (602) 774-3358.

The Museum of Northern Arizona. Three miles north of Flagstaff on US-180 at Fort Valley Road. From downtown Flagstaff, follow the signs to the Grand Canyon via US-180. A small jewel for people interested in knowing about northern Arizona — especially the Navajo and Hopi cultures — the museum offers an outstanding rug display and gift shop. During July, the Hopi and Navajo showcase traditional arts and activities on the beautiful museum grounds. Route 4, Box 720, Flagstaff, AZ 86001. Open daily. Fee. (602) 774-5211.

Pioneer Historical Museum. Fort Valley Road. From downtown Flagstaff, follow the signs to the Grand Canyon via US-180. The museum is two miles north of town (just a mile before you get to the Museum of Northern Arizona). Operated by the Pioneer Historical Society, the facility is devoted to preserving Arizona's pioneer heritage. All kinds of artifacts depicting pioneer life are on display here. If you want to understand what it was like for those people who settled the area, spend some time here. Donation suggested. Open daily. Box 1968, Flagstaff, AZ 86001. (602) 774-6272.

Walnut Canyon National Monument. Off I-40 east, seven and a half miles east of Flagstaff at the Walnut Canyon turnoff. A beautifully preserved Sinaguan cliff dwelling, Walnut Canyon whispers of bygone centuries. Stop first at the visitors center and decide whether to travel into this time warp by strolling in Rim Walk Trail or hiking down Island Trail, a 185-foot descent. Both provide a splendid view of the 300 small cliff dwellings which are confined within this 400-foot deep canyon. If you choose the more strenuous path, prepare to take your time: it takes twice the effort to ascend as it does to descend. Open daily. Fee. (602) 526-3367.

Fairfield Continental Snow Bowl. (Twenty-eight-mile round-trip). Take A-180 (Humphreys Street) north seven miles. Turn right at Snow Bowl Road and continue climbing up that dirt road another seven miles to the end of the path where you'll see the lodge. Indoor-types can eat at the Snow Bowl snack shop and imbibe at the bar. Weather permitting, the top of the Fairfield Continental Snow Bowl is great for a panoramic view or picnic. A ski lift runs up Mount Humphreys, Arizona's highest peak, which towers over the San Francisco Mountain range, during the summer months so that skiers and nonskiers alike can enjoy the view. (602) 526-3232.

WHERE TO EAT

Flagstaff has numerous good restaurants where you can get anything from a juicy hamburger to an elegant meal. Ask the Flagstaff Chamber of Commerce for a brochure with a complete listing. Stop in at the Chamber office, 101 West Santa Fe Ave., Flagstaff, AZ 86001, or call (602) 774-4505.

Black Bart's Steak House. 2760 E. Butler Ave., Flagstaff. This is a good family place featuring steaks and chicken, cowboy beans and biscuits. See the old time review put on by the waiters and waitresses. You'll pay extra for the show but it's worth it. $$; □. (602) 779-3142.

WHERE TO STAY

All kinds of accommodations await tourists. Choose from bed and breakfast and rustic cabins to modern motels and resorts. Check with the Chamber of Commerce, 101 West Santa Fe Ave., Flagstaff, AZ 86001, or call (602) 774-4505 for a complete listing of hotels, motels, and other accommodations.

Little America. Butler Avenue and I-40. This is a large (248-room) facility. The rooms are big and well-appointed, and the bathrooms are luxurious and equipped with telephones. You have several dining rooms to choose from. $$; □. (602) 779-2741 or 1-800-528-1234.

Day Trip 1

CAVE CREEK
CAREFREE
BARTLETT LAKE

CAVE CREEK

This day trip begins at Cave Creek and offers a peek into the not-so-distant past. Along the way, you see the Phoenix urban area at its most posh. Comfortable distances and good shopping make this a relaxing, easy trip. As you travel, you may see "Save Our Desert" signs. These aren't just grafitti. Developers have discovered northeast Phoenix, and houses are stealing the scene from the saguaros. Fortunately, the vast Tonto National Forest is just an arrowhead's throw away. Although this close-in desert is fast disappearing, remember that Arizona is only 18 percent privately owned. Since most of the land belongs to the state and federal governments, hopefully much of it will be saved for posterity.

Cave Creek is a funky little old town which has resisted urban flash, unlike its sister city, Carefree, which was built to attract the well-heeled. A mining camp in the 1880s and a ranching community after the mines gave out, today Cave Creek offers city dwellers an alternative to urban life. Keep your eye out for antique shops. There are some intriguing places to browse. To get to Cave Creek, follow I-17 to the Carefree Highway eastbound. Turn east. It becomes Desert Foothills Drive. Individuals who cared about the desert made the 101 signs identifying the desert plants along the road. As you maneuver the dips, take time to notice these identifying markers and learn about the unusual environment.

WHERE TO EAT

The Horny Toad. 6738 E. Cave Creek Rd., Cave Creek. This is a *gen-u-ine western joint.* Fried chicken (lots of it) is a specialty and its hamburgers are great. Lunch and dinner served daily. $$; □. (602) 488-9542.

    Satisfied Frog. 6245 E. Cave Creek Rd., Cave Creek. Just up the street from The Horny Toad, this restaurant serves equally delicious food. Lunch and dinner, featuring western fare, are served daily. $$; □. (602) 488-3317.

CAREFREE

Another 1950's Arizona phenomenon, Carefree was a real estate developer's dream planned to lure those who have the means and the time to enjoy their leisure. Continue east on Cave Creek Road a mile or so and you're there. The street names say it all — Easy Street, Nonchalant Avenue, Ho and Hum streets, Rocking Chair Road. Carefree is an elegant, little community of large homes, green golf courses and busy boutiques set like jewels into rocky bezels.

WHERE TO GO

The Sundial. Go east on Cave Creek Road to Sunshine Way and turn right. You'll see the sundial right ahead of you. This is the largest sundial in the western hemisphere and a Carefree landmark.

    The Carefree Inn. Mule Train Road, Carefree. Follow the Carefree Highway to Scottsdale Road also called Tom Darlington Drive in Carefree. Turn left and go to Cave Creek Road. Turn right. Continue on this road 1¼ miles and turn left onto Mule Train. About 1¼ miles further on to the left is the Carefree Inn. For years it was the only resort in the area. Recently it's been joined by other elegant places. You can walk around the grounds, eat at the restaurant, browse through the gift shop, or mentally file this place away as a future overnight vacation spot. $$; □. (602) 488-3551.

    The Spanish Village. Carefree. Follow Tom Darlington Drive (Scottsdale Road) south to the signs for "shopping." Wander the narrow streets trimmed with wrought-iron and poke through the art and gift shops. On hot summer days, the inside mall is cool and inviting.

WHERE TO EAT

The Boulders Resort & Club. In Carefree. Head south on Tom Darlington Drive (Scottsdale Road) and turn left just prior to the pile of boulders. Follow the signs to the Boulders Resort & Club. For a real treat, plan a lunch or dinner at the Boulders Club or either of the two restaurants on the grounds. Reservations are required. Don't expect to. drive in simply to look around, because the Boulders carefully protects the privacy of its guests. You won't get past the gatehouse unless you have called ahead to make an appointment or a reservation for a meal. Closed during the summer. Lunch and dinner available at the resort and the club. $$-$$$; . (602) 254-9429.

BARTLETT LAKE

Bartlett Lake. Continue east on Cave Creek Road about six miles. You'll see a fork in the road and a sign to Bartlett Dam Road. Follow the road to the right. It's unimproved, which means dirt, but if you want an adventurous drive, it's for you. These last miles are the roughest. As your teeth jounce inside your mouth, you may wonder why this section of the road isn't paved. You'll understand when you reach this relatively quiet and undisturbed body of water. Boaters and fishermen love keeping Bartlett Lake somewhat inaccessible. It gives them acres of skiable water, virtually untouched by too many other human feet. If you decide to make this trip, know at the outset that the lake is the attraction. Outside of a ranger station, there are no facilities here. That's the allure — rustic beauty unmarred by concession stands.

To return to Phoenix, retrace your steps. Follow Bartlett Lake Road to Cave Creek Road and turn south on Scottsdale Road to Scottsdale. From there, it's an easy trip back to Phoenix via Lincoln Drive and Camelback, Indian School or Thomas roads.

Day Trip 2

PAYSON
TONTO NATURAL BRIDGE
KOHL'S RANCH
WORTH MORE TIME:
CHRISTOPHER CREEK AND WOODS CANYON LAKE

PAYSON

Beginning with Payson, this excursion features a scenic Arizona highway, elegant in every season. You'll cross the Fort McDowell Indian Reservation, enter the Tonto National Forest, climb through the Mazatal Mountains and ultimately experience the carved cliffs and dramatic landscape of the Mogollon Rim country. This is an excellent summer getaway and a "must see" in the autumn. In winter, you'll see cars loaded with ski equipment as families head for the Sunrise ski area. Your main destination is Payson, considered the "Festival Capital" of Arizona. Payson can thank Zane Grey and Grizzly Adams for some of its fame, but nobody can beat Mother Nature for good press.

To reach Payson, head northeast on the Beeline Highway (A-87) — it's right near the border of Scottsdale and Mesa on your map. After crossing the Indian reservation, you'll enter the Tonto National Forest. The road will begin to twist and turn, and you'll pass Sunflower and Rye. Thirteen miles later, you'll reach Payson. Located in the exact center of the state in the world's largest stand of ponderosa pines, Payson sits at 5000 feet and is a sportsman's paradise.

Founded in 1881 as a gold mining camp, Payson counts tourism as its number one industry. Payson hosts a myriad of festivals. Stop in at the Chamber of Commerce, at Beeline Highway and Main Street, to pick up maps and information on what's doing.

WHERE TO GO

The Swiss Village. A-87 on the north side of Payson. Friendly people, gingerbread architecture, a good doughnut shop and lots of gift shops make this a good shopping and refreshment stop.

Zane Grey's Cabin. At the junction of A-260 and A-87. Turn right on A-260 and travel about 20 miles northeast. You'll see a sign to Zane Grey's Cabin and Fish Hatchery just beyond Kohl's Ranch. Turn left, and take that road up the mountain about four and a half miles. Follow the signs and turn left onto a gravel road leading to the restored cabin. It's open from March 1 to November 30 (closed for the snowy winter). Fee. (602) 478-4243.

TONTO NATURAL BRIDGE

About 12 miles north of Payson on A-87, the world's largest travertine natural bridge arches 183 feet above the stream bed. Measuring 150 to 400 feet in width, it is composed of travertine, white limestone, and red coral deposits. The area is laced with ancient Indian caves. This facility is privately owned.

WHERE TO GO

Tonto Creek Falls. A half mile above the junction of Tonto and Horton creeks, 20 miles north of Payson, is the site of this natural waterfall. The area around Payson is studded with sylvan splendor, so stop for a cool respite in a busy day of sightseeing.

WHERE TO STAY

Tonto Natural Bridge Lodge. At the bridge. Call ahead for reservations because accommodations are extremely limited. The facility has just 10 rooms. Write to the Tonto Natural Bridge Lodge, Tonto Natural Bridge, P. O. Box 1600, Pine, AZ 85544. Open all year, weather permitting. $$; no cards. (602) 476-3440.

KOHL'S RANCH

Known for its rustic elegance, Kohl's Ranch is a favorite with locals and visitors. Turn right onto A-260 at the junction of A-87 and A-260 and continue 17 miles to the ranch. Be sure to call ahead for breakfast, lunch or dinner at this longtime Payson landmark. While you're there, enjoy Tonto Creek which runs through the property. If you have time for a quiet retreat at this rustic lodge, burrow in for a weekend in one of the cabins that dot the property. $-$$; □. Use the toll free number from Phoenix: (602) 271-9731; in Payson, (602) 478-4211.

WORTH MORE TIME:
CHRISTOPHER CREEK AND WOODS CANYON LAKE

Hikers and outdoor types will want to continue east another hour on A-260 to see Christopher Creek and Woods Canyon Lake. Both destinations offer excellent opportunities for camping, fishing, boating and hiking.

Or you may prefer to head north on A-87 another 15 to 20 miles to see the towns of Strawberry and, just three miles away, its neighbor, Pine. Both communities are nestled in spectacular woodsy settings and offer travelers a taste of rural, rustic Arizona at its best. Although Strawberry has the oldest standing schoolhouse in the state, most tourists come for the views rather than specific sights. If you decide to visit the area, Strawberry is a good place to stop for available facilities. Both Strawberry and Pine are geared to handle visitors.

From Payson, take A-87 south for a direct return to Phoenix. Or branch off on A-188 toward Punkin Center and Roosevelt Lake and return on the Apache Trail (A-88) past Tortilla Flat, and on into Mesa, Tempe, and Phoenix. This is a secondary road and part of it is unpaved. The Apache Trail is reknowned for its elegant scenery. However if you come home this back way, you're in for some steep climbing, and curvy driving on a gravel road. (Refer to Day Trip 1, EAST FROM PHOENIX, for more informaton about the area.)

Day Trip 3

SALT RIVER RECREATION CENTER
SAGUARO LAKE

SALT RIVER RECREATION CENTER SAGUARO LAKE

For a real change of pace, take a short drive and a long float down the river. Drive north on A-87 to the Saguaro (Sa-wa-ro) Lake cutoff (Bush Highway). Follow the signs past the entrance to Saguaro Lake and the Salt River Recreation Center.

Saguaro Lake was formed by Stewart Mountain Dam and is one of several lakes built for water reclamation purposes. You can find out all about tubing at the central office, including where to get in and out on the Salt River. Tubing is fast becoming Arizona's state sport, as a visit to the Blue Point area of the Salt River will attest on any hot day. Wear shorts or a bathing suit and tennies; pack beverages and an inner tube (or rent one there). Bring sunscreen, friends, rope, and styrofoam cooler that you can lash to an extra tube and a hat or visor if the day is extremely warm. Be prepared for some gentle, but exciting, rapids. While the water is rarely deep, tubers can get into trouble if they don't pay attention to the rocks and snags. Tubing is a great way to spend a day from May through September. To check on river conditions, call (602) 984-3305.

If getting wet and wild doesn't appeal to you, follow the signs to Saguaro Lake for a more peaceful view of water life.

WHERE TO GO

The Saguaro Lake Marina. Rent a boat to fully enjoy a day on the lake. Call the Arizona Marine Office, (602) 982-5546.

Saguaro Lake Excursion. Cruise the lake on a paddle boat. Fee. For schedule information, call (602) 892-2799.

Usery Mountain Park. At Bush Highway and Usery Pass Road. Continue on Bush Highway to Usery Pass Road. Turn left onto Usery Pass Road and follow it for two or three miles to this elegant mountain park. Spend time hiking the well-marked nature trails, or riding (if you trailer in your own horses). This is one of the nicest mountain parks "out in the tullies."

WHERE TO EAT

Lake Shore Inn Restaurant. At the Saguaro Lake Marina. A full-service menu features down-home fare. Come for biscuits and gravy at breakfast, barbecued chicken and sandwiches at lunch, and steaks and seafood at dinner. Call for hours. $$. □. (602) 984-5311.

Saguaro Lake Guest Ranch. 13020 Bush Hwy., Mesa, AZ 85205. Call ahead and make reservations for breakfast, lunch or dinner. You can also arrange for trail rides or float trips (guided or unguided) down the Salt River. This guest ranch offers 25 rustic cottages (each holds two to four persons comfortably) and a host of planned outings from fishing to overnight pack trips. $$; American Express only. (602) 984-2194.

Day Trip 1

SCOTTSDALE

SCOTTSDALE

No trip around Phoenix is complete without a day in Scottsdale. Famous as "The West's Most Western Town," Scottsdale is the shopping and art hub of the Valley of the Sun. It's difficult to believe that only a few decades ago Scottsdale Road was unpaved and cowboys rode into town on Saturday night to whoop it up. Today it's a gathering spot for art aficionados, dedicated shoppers and gourmets.

Follow Glendale Avenue east to Scottsdale. North of Central Avenue, Glendale becomes Lincoln Drive. Continue east on Lincoln Drive and, as you near 24th Street and Lincoln, look to your left. There's Squaw Peak, one of Phoenix's in-town mountain parks. Fit Phoenicians routinely climb Squaw Peak — some do this daily. If you have time and good walking shoes, turn toward the mountain at the sign to the park and explore a bit.

Continue on Lincoln Drive to Scottsdale Road. You'll pass through the town of Paradise Valley (not to be confused with the Paradise Valley area of Phoenix). This is a wealthy residential community of one-acre-plus homesites and a few well-manicured resorts. Paradise Valley is nestled between Mummy Mountain to the north and Camelback Mountain to the south.

Turn south onto Scottsdale Road and head into town for shopping and browsing. Later, you'll drive north to see other attractions. Scottsdale prides itself on its thriving downtown, outstanding art galleries and variety of fine restaurants. During the tourist season (October through April) be prepared for traffic.

Scottsdale is named for General Winfield Scott, and, although it has only come of age as a city in the last 25 years, the town has long been a vacation spot. Turn-of-the-century residents used to rent out rooms and screened sleeping porches to visitors who passed through. An independent place, Scottsdale's civic history is punctuated with innovation and creativity. City fathers got on the urban redevelopment bandwagon early and turned a run-down section into a showcase for business and government. They were also instrumental in developing flood-prone Indian Bend Wash into a series of green city parks and lakes. Today this beautiful, nationally acclaimed wash runs the entire length of town along Hayden Boulevard. Every day of the year you can find activity there — from roller skating, fishing and soccer to volleyball, baseball and jogging.

WHERE TO GO

Fifth Avenue

As you head south on Scottsdale Road, turn west onto Fifth Avenue (there's a light). Drive slowly and look for a free parking space anywhere along the street. The city also maintains several free lots. This shopping area is replete with unusual boutiques and gift shops. Fifth Avenue continues quite a distance and ultimately meets Indian School Road, a main east-west thoroughfare. Best advice is to bring plenty of cash and be ready to browse.

Craftsman's Court. Running south from Fifth Avenue, one block west of Scottsdale Road, is Craftsman's Court. If you don't know it's there, you can miss this charming section. Walk down this narrow short street to discover specialty shops and a quaint patio setting.

Marshall Way. Intersects with Fifth Avenue, one block west of Craftsman's Court. Marshall Way is a unique street. Some places to visit here include:

Seeger's Gallery. 4200 N. Marshall Way. Go in and see the "Seeger People." Dick Seeger, a long time Scottsdale artist, has been doing unusual work with plastics for years. Then he combined his photographic and artistic skills to come up with one-of-a-kind portraits. He'll pose you and take your photograph. Then he mounts your favorites on plastic, cuts them out (almost like a paperdoll), and positions them on a lucite base to create unique three-dimensional sculptures. You need to see these to get the full impact. Even if you're not a portrait candidate, you'll find lots to intrigue you in his gallery. Incidentally, "Seeger People" is a patented concept so you'll only see it here. (602) 949-1130.

The Gallery Wall. 7051 Fifth Ave. (The address is misleading. The entrance is on Marshall Way.) This gallery is the only representative of two nationally recognized American artists, Allan Houser and Dan Naminga. Houser, an Apache, is a sculptor whose work in stone and bronze portray the Indian but speak to all races. Naminga, a Hopi, is primarily known for his expressive, colorful canvases which capture the essence of the mesas where he grew up. Owners Sandy and Glenn Green will be happy to tell you about Allan and Dan. The Gallery Wall is also in Santa Fe, and a framing operation is in Phoenix. (602) 990-9110.

The Hand and the Spirit Crafts Gallery. 4222 N. Marshal Way. More a mini-museum than a crafts gallery, The Hand and the Spirit features nationally recognized craftsmen. Shows are held for artists. If you enjoy seeing the best in sophisticated contemporary crafts, this is the place for you. (602) 949-1262.

Ex Libris Art Books. 4222 N. Marshall Way. Where else but in Scottsdale will you find an entire bookstore dedicated to books on art — in all its various forms? There is also a fine selection of gift items including a collection from the Museum of Modern Art in New York. Great for browsing and buying. (602) 941-5289.

Minds Eye Contemporary Crafts. 4200 N. Marshall Way. Outstanding Arizona and Southwestern craftspeople are featured here in a dazzling display of different styles, textures and designs. You can experience an impressive variety of art objects — hand-painted clothing to sculptures to earrings to pottery. This is a great place to pick up a special "Arizona" something for yourself or to send back home. (602) 941-2494.

Gallery 10. 7045 3rd Ave. Continue on Marshall to 3rd Avenue to this low cluster of adobe buildings. Native American art and contemporary Southwestern art are featured in this elegant gallery, which shows works by prominent artists, including Paul Pletka. (602) 994-0405.

Elaine Horwitch Gallery. 4201 N. Marshall Way. This gallery features fine contemporary Arizona and Southwestern artists. If Elaine isn't there, she may be in her Sedona or Santa Fe gallery. Shows change frequently, so visit often. (602) 945-0791.

WHERE TO EAT

Al Fresco Patio Cafe. 7051 5th Ave. Next to By George, a unique gift shop, this tucked-away patio restaurant serves great homemade sandwiches and delicious salads. Have a quick or leisurely lunch on the shady patio. If you're still hungry, there's a Haägan Dazs right there as well. Lunch only. $$; no cards. (602) 941-1111.

Main Street

During your stroll through the Fifth Avenue area, be sure to wander along Stetson Drive, 70th Street and 6th Avenue as well. Once you have covered Fifth Avenue, you're ready to move on to Main Street. Main Street is lined with galleries, and this area, more than any other in Scottsdale, reflects the city's emphasis on the arts. More than 90 galleries serve a town of 100,000 and you quickly realize that paintings, sculpture and crafts are big business here.

To reach Main Street, drive east on Fifth Avenue to Scottsdale Road. Turn south on Scottsdale Road and turn west at Main Street. Later you'll turn east to vistit Old Town Scottsdale and its Western shops.

WHERE TO GO

You'll notice immediately that Scottsdale's Old Town area projects an "Old Western" image. The pedestrian crossing areas are set off in simulated brick, and the sidewalks along Main Street are shaded by wooden-shingled porticos extending from the buildings. These serve a practical, as well as an aesthetic purpose. During the hot summer months, when temperatures climb upwards to 110 degrees, the roofs afford essential shade.

Park free anywhere on Main Street. If you arrive in Scottsdale during the tourist season (October through April), do attend one of the Thursday evening art walks. Every Thursday night during the fall, winter and spring months, galleries host open houses and openings.

Art enthusiasts will discover that Main Street represents a good mix of styles and schools. Many collectors visit Scottsdale because of its fine Western galleries, including Main Trail, El Prado, Golden West Galleries and The May Gallery. In addition, you can browse through fine contemporary, Native American and graphic art galleries for artifacts, home accessories and antiques — all are well represented here. If leather clothing is your thing, Lord Latigo at 7177 E. Main St. is a must.

As you cross Scottsdale Road, heading east on Main Street, another world opens — one dedicated to the old West. Park on Main Street East of Scottsdale Road, walk east to Brown Avenue and then turn north. This area is a mecca for tourists; shops range from junk to funk — with some fine jewelry and clothing shops featuring Western wear tossed in for good measure.

Stroll north on Brown Street toward Indian School Road for more shopping or browsing at Pima Plaza. Located on First Avenue between Scottsdale Road and Brown, Pima Plaza has restaurants, art galleries and unusual shops, including one completely devoted to music boxes.

Civic Center Mall

The Civic Center Mall area backs up to Old Town. Once a rundown section of Scottsdale, it is now a source of pride. The government complex includes the Scottsdale City Hall, City Court, Library and Center for the Arts, all designed by local architect Bennie Gonzales. The rolling lawns of the mall also act as an outdoor art museum for an impressive collection of contemporary sculpture.

WHERE TO GO

The Scottsdale Library. 3839 Civic Center Plaza. Stop in to enjoy the architecture and ambience. Visit the Arizona room as well. Here you'll see displays featuring Arizona history — from rare books to silver saddles.

The Scottsdale Center for the Arts. 7383 Scottsdale Mall. This facility boasts a theatre for the performing arts and visual arts gallery. Both the theatre and gallery feature outstanding, nationally-known artists. In addition, the Scottsdale Arts Center Association sponsors special events during the year, including an outdoor crafts show. There's also a small, unique gallery shop for browsing. Open Tuesday to Sunday. Admission to the Center is free but performances and exhibits often have fees. Check with the box office for schedules. (602) 992-ARTS.

The Lovena Ohl Gallery. 4251 Marshall Way. If you want to see the finest in Native American art, this is the place. The gallery is tucked away near Chez Louie and not visible from the street. You can park free in the city parking lot, Second Avenue between Brown Street and Civic Center Plaza, and walk through the mall to the gallery.

Lovena Ohl is an Arizona tradition. Years before Indian jewelry and artwork became fashionable, she sought out young, unknown artists on the reservation and brought their artwork to the attention of discriminating collectors. She operated the gift shop at the Heard Museum in Phoenix for many years before opening her own gallery. Now she's added another star to her career — a scholarship awarded each year to an artist to enable him or her to spend a year attaining a special dream. Lovena features the work of such acclaimed artists as Charles Loloma, Larry Golsh, Harvey Begay, Tony Da and James Little. (602) 945-8212. (See directions to Marshall Way on p.44.)

Trailside Galleries. 7330 Scottsdale Mall. Western art lovers will find much to enjoy at this gallery where a variety of works by important artists is featured. There's also a fine print gallery. (602) 945-7751.

Once you've had your fill of boutique shopping, drive north on Scottsdale Road to Camelback and turn west. Both the Camelview Plaza Mall, at 70th Street and Camelback Street, and Scottsdale Fashion Square, at Scottsdale Road and Camelback, offer some of the valley's finest department stores and specialty shops.

The Borgata

For a taste of Rodeo Drive, Arizona style, continue north on Scottsdale Road to one traffic light north of McDonald Drive. You'll see what looks like a fortress on the left. This is the Borgata. (When it was new, locals called it "Fort Ostentatious," but since then it has won the hearts and minds of all.) It was designed to resemble an ancient Italian village. Why Italy in the midst of Arizona? Who knows? As you stroll the interior brick courtyard, you'll find a clutch of Arizona's — and the world's — most chic shops. You'll love the atmosphere.

Later on, round out your day with a visit to The Cosanti Foundation and Taliesin West, north on Scottsdale Road. Finish up with some Arizona mountain scenery on your way to Fountain Hills, a scenic planned community, where you'll see the world's tallest fountain.

WHERE TO GO

The Cosanti Foundation. 6433 Doubletree Ranch Rd., Paradise Valley. As you leave the Borgata, go north on Scottsdale Road to Dobletree Ranch Road at the fourth stoplight. Turn west and watch for the sign to The Cosanti Foundation on the south side fo the street. Wander through Paolo Soleri's enchanted studio. You'll be fascinated by the Soleri wind chimes. Made and sold on the premises, they make wonderful Arizona keepsakes. You also can ask to see the scale model for Arcosanti, the prototype community which Soleri is building in the desert north of Phoenix. Open daily. Donation suggested. (602) 948-6145.

Taliesin West. Taliesin West, Scottsdale, AZ 85261. Scottsdale Road to Shea Boulevard. Turn east on Shea for about four miles and make a left at N. 106th St. (also called Via Linda). Go approximately 0.4 miles and turn left at N. 108th St. Follow that to Taliesin West.

Taliesin West is the headquarters for Taliesin Associated Architects and an architectural school teaching the design principles and philosophy of the late Frank Lloyd Wright, one of America's most respected architects. Wright died in 1959, but his belief that environment and structure should blend into a total harmony continues to influence architects throughout the world.

"Under construction" since the 1930s Taliesin West has been built and maintained by professionals and students who live and work there. (The original Taliesin was built in Wisconsin in the early 1900s.) The structures serve as a living testimony to Wright's enduring genius.

The compound is constructed of native Arizona materials. The main building is positioned and designed to take full advantage of the warm winter sun. Hour-long tours given by Taliesin staff and students are available daily. These talks are exceptionally informative. Closed during the summer. Call for information. Fee. (602) 948-6670.

Rawhide. 23023 N. Scottsdale Rd. On Scottsdale Road, four miles north of Bell Road. Privately owned, this authentic 1880s town is a great stop for families. It has shops, a museum, ice cream parlor, stage coach ride and much more. If you visit during July and August, wear a hat because the "town" is hot and dusty. You'll get a real appreciation for the Arizona pioneers. They did it all without the benefit of nearby ice cream parlors and cold beer! See the Conestoga wagon and hear the story of what it was like to come West. Admission is free, but fees are charged for various rides and activities. Open daily. (602) 536-5111.

WHERE TO EAT

Scottsdale has a full complement of superb restaurants. A sampling of some area favorites.

Around Main Street

The Sugar Bowl Ice Cream Parlor. 4005 N. Scottsdale Rd. Nationally known cartoonist Bil Keene (he resides in Paradise Valley) refers to this Scottsdale landmark. The pink decor is vintage ice cream parlor and the sundaes, sodas and other concoctions are always top-notch. Ice cream is served until 11 p.m. $; no cards. (602) 946-0051.

Daa's Thai Room. 7419 Indian Plaza. One-half block south of Camelback Road and approximately one-half mile east of Scottsdale Road. Home-cooked Thai food at its best. A word of warning: it's hot and spicy! $$; □. (602) 941-9015.

Kyoto. 7170 E. Stetson Ave. South of Camelback Road and west of Scottsdale Road. When you have a yen for Japanese, this is the place for a sushi bar and steak house. Wonderful atmosphere and always a good fresh list of sushi choices. $$; □. (602) 990-9374.

Los Olivos Mexican Patio. 7328 Second St. The entrance is just north off Second Street and one block east of Scottsdale Road. Park in the free city parking structure there. Start with a cheese crisp for an appetizer and go from there. If you're new to Mexican food, the chunky salsa is milder. There's music and dancing on weekends. $-$$; □. (602) 946-2256.

Avanti. 3102 N. Scottsdale Rd. Just south of Thomas Road and south of the downtown area. A glossy black and white interior and elegant continental menu make this a favorite. Like most of the better Scottsdale establishments, jackets are *not* required for gentlemen. $$-$$$; □. (602) 949-8333.

Around Fashion Square

The Duck and Decanter. 6900 E. Camelback Rd., in Camelview Plaza Mall. Take the escalator upstairs for an indoor "outdoor" patio experience. Your sandwich comes brown-bagged. Along with your sandwich or salad, you'll find a plate, utensils, pickles and a candy treat. Continental breakfast is available in the morning. Stop for lunch or afternoon tea. Famous for sandwiches, salads and flavored teas, and the duck is always delicious. $$; □. (602) 941-3896.

In The Borgata

Kron Chocolatier. 6166 N. Scottsdale Rd. Stop in for a sample — there's always an inviting candy dish. Treat yourself royally to a gourmet chocolate confection. $-$$; □. (602) 998-5967.

WHERE TO EAT

Handlebar-J. 7116 E. Becker Lane. One block northwest of Shea Boulevard off Scottsdale Road. Good for steaks and ribs plus live country music, this is a place locals frequent. Tourists should try the house special drink. $$; □. (602) 948-0110.

Rawhide. 23023 N. Scottsdale Rd. Head north on Scottsdale Road, four miles north of Bell Road. Steaks, chicken and ribs are served in a Western dance hall atmosphere. $$; □. (602) 563-5111.

Pinnacle Peak Patio. 8655 East Via De Ventura. Take Scottsdale Road north to Pinnacle Peak Road; turn east on Pinnacle Peak to where it dead-ends into Via De Ventura. Go north on Via De Ventura. You can't miss the huge rambling complex which is famous for mesquite broiled steaks, as well as cutting off the neckties of unsuspecting "dudes" who come into a cowboy place too dressed up. There's indoor seating for 2400 and outdoor accommodations for nearly 6000. If you take an unsuspecting friend, make sure he has on an old tie because Pinnacle Peak Patio is merciless. (After the tie is cut, it is displayed along with the owner's business card.) Stay for dancing to live cowboy music, or walk off your dinner by strolling around the grounds or browsing in the shops. $$; . Open daily. (602) 949-7311.

Reata Pass Steak House. Star Route. Follow Scottsdale Road north to Pinnacle Peak Road and head east on Pinnacle Peak to where it dead-ends into Via De Ventura. Go north on Via De Ventura and you will see Reata Pass on your left, just before you get to Pinnacle Peak Patio. You'll find mesquite-broiled steaks, chicken and ribs served here in a slightly more intimate, yet rugged, setting. This is worth the drive for the good food, live country music and great desert views. Reservations encouraged. $$; □. (602) 563-5220.

Oaxaca at Pinnacle Peak Village. 8711 E. Pinnacle Peak Rd., Scottsdale, AZ 85255. Drive north on Scottsdale Road to Pinnacle Peak Road and head east on Pinnacle Peak to the Village at Pinnacle Peak. Go upstairs and if the weather permits, ask for seating on the patio. Fresh fish is their specialty along with spectacular views. $$. □. (602) 998-2222.

Vincent's. 8711 E. Pinnacle Peak Rd., Scottsdale, AZ 85255. Downstairs from Oaxaca, feast on gourmet French and Continental cuisine. Save room for dessert. The pastries are out of this world. $$-$$$. □. (602) 998-0921.

The Palm Court. 7700 E. McCormick Parkway in Scottsdale. Award-winning elegance and gourmet dining at its finest are available at the Scottsdale Conference Center Resort. Great atmosphere. $$$; □. (602) 991-3400.

Day Trip 2

TEMPE
MESA
APACHE JUNCTION
TORTILLA FLAT
THE LAKES

TEMPE

The East Valley is booming. Just 15 years ago, most of eastern metropolitan Phoenix was open space. Snowbirds, or winter visitors, as they are more politely called, flocked to the east valley in cold weather. Farms flourished and although small towns hinted that one day they would become urban centers, such amazing growth seemed light-years away. Cotton was king, but much of that is history now. As you drive out of Mesa toward Tortilla Flat you'll pass through an unrelenting wave of development for the first few miles.

New homes and businesses sprout faster than any crop out here. Consequently, as you leave the urban area behind and continue along the famous Apache Trail, you'll marvel at the wild natural beauty so near the city. When your day is done, you'll even know the answer to those ubiquitous bumper stickers which ask: "Where the Hell is Tortilla Flat?"

Tempe once was a sleepy little college town. No more. Today it is the home of one of the nation's largest universities — Arizona State. Originally called "Hayden's Ferry," Tempe has a history that's liberally sprinkled with famous Arizona names. The town owes its past, present and future to Judge Trumbell Hayden, a miller, educator and all-around promoter, who established a ferry across the Salt River in 1872. A community, which quickly followed, became known as Tempe by

51

1877. Almost immediately, Judge Hayden began lobbying the territorial government to establish a teacher's college in Tempe. That tiny college grew up to be Arizona State University (ASU).

Today Tempe continues to be a pioneer community. The city is involved in building one of the initial demonstration projects for a redeveloped Salt River which is part of a metropolitan-wide Rio Salado project. Twice a year the town hosts a superb crafts festival along Mill Avenue. And, of course, it continues to be proud of its home-town school, ASU.

If you want to see the campus, park in one of the visitors' lots and walk around the palm-lined malls. When school's in session, parking is tight — you'll understand why parking is the bane of the 1980s college student's existence.

To get a sense of Tempe's past and future, drive through the quaint downtown. Follow Mill Avenue south past Gammage Center for the Performing Arts. You may wish to make a quick jog east to see Tempe City Hall at 31 East Fifth St. Turn east off Mill Avenue onto East Fifth for a short half block to get a glimpse of this unusual contemporary structure. Designed in the shape of an inverted pyramid, the glass and steel building shades itself from the glaring Arizona sun.

WHERE TO GO

Arizona State University Gammage Center for the Performing Arts. On the corner of Mill Avenue and Apache Boulevard. This was the last building Frank Lloyd Wright designed. Although he did not live to see it completed, it's a hallmark of Wright's vision. Follow Scottsdale Road south into Tempe where it becomes Rural Road. Turn west onto University Drive and south on Mill. You'll see the center's distinctive pink color and scalloped roofline just beyond the curve on Mill between University and Apache. The public may purchase tickets to events at Gammage. There's a full season of music, dance, theatre and lectures. To inquire about scheduled events, write the Gammage Box Office, Arizona State University, Tempe, AZ 85287. Half-hour tours of the building are available on a limited basis. Call for times and days. Free. (602) 965-5062.

If you want to spend more time on campus, pick up a map from an attendant at any of the visitors' parking lots. The map will direct you to other points of interest.

MESA

To get to Mesa from Tempe, follow Apache Boulevard east. As it enters Mesa, Apache becomes Main Street. Once known primarily for its wide streets — wide enough for an ox team to turn around — Mesa today competes with Phoenix as an urban and cultural hub. The fast-growing city is proud of its excellent schools and churches; recently, it has been taking an active role in the arts, as well. The Chamber of Commerce, 10 W. 1st St., has information on the community center, historical and archaelogical museum, little theatres and youth museum. (602) 969-1307.

WHERE TO GO

The Mormon Temple. 525 East Main St. — Apache Boulevard (US-60 and 89) becomes Main Street in Mesa. This imposing structure serves as Arizona headquarters for the Church of Jesus Christ of Latter-day Saints. Although the sanctuary is open only to Mormons, the visitors center welcomes guests. There you may learn something about the Mormon faith and hear about the Mormon men and women who came west to establish homes, farms and communities. Tours of the Temple grounds are conducted every half hour. Call for more information. (602) 964-7164.

APACHE JUNCTION

Continue east on US-60-89 to Apache Junction, which calls itself "the gateway to the Superstition Mountains." This range has fascinated people for almost a century, ever since the German immigrant Jacob Waltz arrived in Arizona in 1863 to prospect for gold. According to legend, Waltz found, or possibly stole, one of the very rich Peralta gold mines deep in the Superstitions. However, try as he did, he never was able to find the mine and prove his claim.

Because people mistakenly thought that the immigrant was from Holland, as Waltz continued his search, the story grew about the "Dutchman's Lost Mine." In time, the unproven claim became known as "The Lost Dutchman's Mine," a misstatement that no one has bothered to correct.

Apache Junction itself is a sprawling conglomeration of commercial property and mobile homes set against the spectacular Superstition range. Drive through Apache Junction and continue on A-88 to begin the Apache Trail, a section of Arizona that quite impressed President Theodore Roosevelt. Observing that it combined the grandeur of the Alps, the glory of the Rockies and the magnificence of the Grand Canyon, he called it "the most awe-inspiring and most sublimely beautiful panorama Nature has ever created." Teddy Roosevelt predicted in 1911 that the Salt River Valley would boom and attract people from throughout the country.

WHERE TO EAT

The Mining Camp Restaurant. 1600 East Mining Camp Rd., Apache Junction. Turn left onto A-88 at Apache Junction and continue north for four miles. The restaurant is a long-time landmark which offers never-ending amounts of hearty Western food amidst a rustic gold-mining atmosphere. Dinner only. $$; □. (602) 982-3181.

TORTILLA FLAT

Travel 18 miles northeast on A-88 to reach Tortilla Flat, one of the last true outposts of the West. Here visitors will find a rustic dining room featuring hamburgers and chili, a weatherbeaten-looking small hotel, and a public restroom.

Although tiny by anyone's standards, Tortilla Flat is the last town between Apache Junction and Roosevelt Dam. A few miles east of Tortilla Flat, the Apache Trail turns into a rough, gravel road. If you decide to continue east to Roosevelt Lake, prepare yourself for a rugged trip.

THE LAKES

If you're ready for more scenery, follow A-88 east 28 miles through the chain of man-made lakes on the Salt River that include Canyon Lake, Apache Lake and Roosevelt Lake, which is much larger than the other two. Roosevelt Lake is located on the gravel road after the pavement ends. The unpaved stretch is notable, not only for its rough surface, but also for its steep descent into Fish Creek Canyon. Adventurous tourists are advised to make this trip by traveling east, not west in order to easily see approaching automobiles.

Fish, water ski, relax, swim or just enjoy the desert lake views. Each lake offers services for travelers.

WHERE TO GO

Canyon Lake. Take the Dolly Steamboat Cruise on a paddlewheeler around the lake. Call (602) 827-9144 for departure times. Fee. For other information call Arizona Marina, (602) 986-0969.

Apache Lake. You'll find a full-service resort and marina with houseboat rentals, boats for fishing and tackle. Check with the Apache Lake Resort for more information. (602) 467-2511.

Roosevelt Lake. A year-round haven for unwinding, popular among skiers, bass fishermen and campers. There's a full-service marina. (602) 467-2245.

Day Trip 3

SUPERIOR
MIAMI-GLOBE
WORTH MORE TIME:
SALT RIVER CANYON AND SHOW LOW

SUPERIOR

Pick up this trip in Apache Junction and travel southeast on US-60-89 toward Superior. The approximately 50-mile drive from Mesa to Superior takes you deep into copper mining country. Arizona owes its history to the mines and the railroads, for the presence of precious minerals — gold, silver and copper — lured people west. The railroads opened the land so that men could carry those treasures out, and, in the process, made the territory accessible to settlers.

The main street of this small town follows Queen Creek, which is nestled among the copper-stained mountains. In 1875, this was a bustling silver and gold mining center. Today its future hangs on a precarious copper balance.

WHERE TO GO

Boyce Thompson Southwestern Arboretum. US-60-89 just a few miles west of Superior. As you drive toward Superior on US-60-89, turn right at the sign and follow the driveway into the arboretum. This vast (1076-acre) living museum was the dream of William Boyce Thompson, a mining magnate and philanthropist. He endowed not only this site, but also a sister institution, the Boyce Thompson Institute for Plant Research on the Cornell University campus in Ithaca, New York. The Arizona arboretum is all the more intriguing because of its Sonoran desert location.

If you have never meandered in a shady and fragrant eucalyptus grove, stared at the myriad of twisted arms of a 200-year-old giant Saguaro cactus, or tried to figure out how the bizarre Boojum tree grows, you've missed some of the desert's best pleasures. Begin your tour at the visitors center, and get acquainted with this living garden before heading out on the well-marked trails. They begin with some "easy-does-it" walks and graduate to more challenging terrain.

One fascinating section is devoted to Old World trees, including the pomegranate, Chinese pistachio and olive, which are of major economic importance in various parts of the world. You will be amazed to learn how many different trees can grow in the Arizona desert. Open daily except Christmas. Fee. (602) 689-2811.

MIAMI-GLOBE

Continue on US-60-89 east to Miami and Globe. As you enter Miami, look for the sign noting the site of the Bloody Tanks Massacre of Apaches. Proceed east to Globe, the seat of Gila County and a center for cattle and mining. Globe began as a mining town in 1886, but now it is the trading center for the San Carlos Apache Indian Reservation and a favorite headquarters for wild pig (javelina) hunting. Apart from the natural setting, the main attraction here is mining. Stop in at the Globe-Miami Chamber of Commerce, 1450 North Broad St., Globe, or call (602) 425-4495 for information on the area.

As in many Arizona small towns, public buildings here often do not have street addresses. However, Arizonans are a friendly bunch so you can always ask directions. You should include the **Gila County Historical Museum** on US-60-89 in your tour. This small museum holds a treasure trove of pioneer and mining artifacts collected throughout the region. It's open daily and is free. No phone. You can see local and regional artists represented at the restored old courthouse, now the **Gila County Arts Museum,** at Broad and Oak streets. This museum is open daily and is free. Then, too, the area is laced with fascinating Pueblo Indian ruins. Ask about them at the Chamber of Commerce.

Group tours of the open pit and smelter operations are available. However if you want to learn more about mining on your own, pick up A-77 at Globe and head south to Winkleman and Hayden, two small copper mining communities which are one mile apart. Here you can hook into DAY TRIP 1, SOUTHEAST FROM PHOENIX by circling through San Manuel to Oracle Junction. At Oracle Junction follow US-89 for a 42-mile drive north to Florence. You can also continue on A-287 from Horace to A-87 back through Chandler to Mesa.

This is a 246-mile drive and much of it traverses old stagecoach routes which are surrounded by massive copper-stained mountains.

WORTH MORE TIME:
SALT RIVER CANYON
& SHOW LOW

From the Miami-Globe area continue northeast on A-77/US-60 another 87 miles for a magnificent plunge through the wild beauty of the Salt River Canyon and a visit to the community of Show Low. You should plan to spend the night in Show Low or head southeast for approximately five miles on A-260 to Lakeside or Pinetop and stay there.

The Salt River Canyon begins about 30 miles northeast of Globe on A-77/US-60 and is often called "the mini Grand Canyon." Take this drive during the daytime so you can appreciate the spectacular sights. The highway twists and turns for five miles from the top of the canyon to its floor.

This is one of the most scenic stretches in all of Arizona. Along the way, you can pull off at several lookout points to admire the artistry wrought by millions of years of erosion. If you have packed a light lunch, you can picnic at one of the several shady spots provided at the bottom of the canyon.

This area is well-marked. Pull off, park and walk down a flight of steps to the river bank. Adventurous adults and children will want to explore the river, swim or fish. If you travel seven miles downstream on a dirt road, you'll see the amazing **Salt Banks.** The formations tower 1000 feet above the river, looking like giant ocean waves frozen in time and about to crest.

When you're ready for the long climb out of the canyon, continue approximately 60 miles northeast on A-77/US-60 to Show Low. This small community is a hub of activity for the 4 million acres of the White Mountain Recreation Area which includes 500 miles of trout streams and 50 lakes. It is also home to **Sunrise Park,** the state's most complete ski center and resort.

Show Low enjoys a high, cool climate and a backdrop of exceptional forestland. Its name came from an incident involving C. E. Cooley, who had been a government scout with Gen. George Crook. Cooley married the daughter of Chief Pedro of the White Mountain Apaches and, in 1875, established a home on what is now called Show Low Creek. His place became a favorite spot for travelers. Marion Clark was Cooley's partner, but at some point in the relationship, Clark decided to end their hotel venture. To settle on who should stay and who should leave, the two agreed to play a card game of Seven-Up. When the hand was dealt, Cooley lacked a single point to win. As they prepared to draw cards, Clark is reputed to have said, "If you can show low, you can win."

Cooly tossed his hand down and said, "Show low it is." Clark moved up the creek to what is now Pinetop, and thanks to the deuce of clubs, Cooley stayed. More importantly, the name stuck.

Today Show Low is the trade and services center for southern Navajo County and portions of southern Apache County. Tourists use it as a jumping-off point for recreation in the White Mountains. You'll find modest facilities here, including motels, cabins and campgrounds. For more information, contact the Show Low Chamber of Commerce, P. O. Box 1083, Show Low, AZ 85901, or call (602) 537-2326.

Day Trip 1

GUADALUPE
SACATON
CASA GRANDE RUINS NATIONAL MONUMENT
FLORENCE

GUADALUPE

Begin by driving east on I-10 to Guadalupe, a primarily Hispanic community south of Phoenix. Guadalupe offers a taste of Old Mexico just a few miles outside of the Phoenix urban center.

WHERE TO GO

Mercado Guadalupe. 9201 S. Avenida Del Yaqui. Follow Avenida Del Yaqui, the main street, through town. You'll see a big blue building. This is the Mercado, or market place, a typical Mexican focal point for shopping and dining. It is located on the corner of Guadalupe Rd. and Avenida Del Yaqui. Most merchants are closed on Wednesday. The Mercado is a great place for gringos to try *authentic* Mexican food. (602) 838-4654.

SACATON

Gila River Indian Crafts Center and Heritage Park. Sacaton. Follow I-10 south to exit 175 which leads to the center. If you have never visited an Indian reservation, this may appear a stark landscape. The attraction here is the **Gila River Indian Crafts Center** which does a brisk business in authentic Indian jewelry of turquoise, silver and

beadwork; pottery from many different tribes; Seri wood carvings:
Navajo rugs; and other gift items. In addition, there's an Indian art
gallery, historical museum, park and a coffee shop featuring piping hot
Indian fry bread. The center is open daily. (602) 963-3981.

CASA GRANDE RUINS NATIONAL MONUMENT

From Sacaton take A-287 southwest for approximately 14 miles to
Coolidge. As you approach Coolidge you will come to the Casa Grande
Ruins National Monument, an 11-room, 11-family, 600-year-old apart-
ment building built by the ancient Hohokam and Pueblo Indian farmers.
This structure was constructed of hardened mud blocks, five feet long,
two feet high and four feet thick and discovered by Father Eusebio
Francisco Kino in 1694. Today it is protected by a giant steel "um-
brella," and its original use is still debated. It may have been a watch-
tower or a religious temple or even an astronomical observatory. Visit
the museum on the site for a closer look at the history of these extraor-
dinary people. Open daily. Fee. (602) 723-3172.

FLORENCE

Continue east on A-287 to Florence, approximately nine miles from
Coolidge. Florence has two main claims to fame: its courthouse and the
prison. The fifth oldest city in the state, it was established in 1866 by a
local Indian agent, Livi Ruggles. The community grew rapidly and
became the county seat when Pinal County was chartered in 1875. In
spite of its desert setting, Florence is an agricultural community. Local
crops include cotton, cattle, sugar beets, grain and grapes.

Poston Butte, named for Charles Poston, the "Father of Arizona," is
a nearby landmark. A monument at the summit of the butte marks his
grave. The town is also known as the "Cowboy Cradle of the
Southwest." During the depression when jobs and money were scarce
and the bottom fell out of the milk market, ranchers were planning to
dump their milk rather than sell it at a loss. A local rancher, Charlie
Whittlow, declared that he would give his milk free to the
schoolchildren rather than waste it. Other communities soon picked up
Whittlow's idea, and as a result, the national milk and free lunch program for school children was started in this country. An odd sidelight to
this story is that while Whittlow was a rancher and *not* a cowboy, as a
result of his actions, his home town became known as "The Cowboy
Cradle of the Southwest."

If you want to continue to Tucson (SEE DAY TRIP 2, SOUTHEAST FROM PHOENIX), you may take US-89 south (Pinal Pioneer Parkway) for a 42-mile scenic stretch between Florence and Oracle Junction and then continue south to Tucson. This drive takes you through a unique natural garden where virtually every type of Arizona desert flora and fauna is displayed. Depending upon your time and botanical interest, you can explore easily accessible side roads along the way.

To return to Phoenix from Florence take US-89 north for 16 miles to its junction with US-60. Turn west and follow US-60/89 47 miles to Phoenix through Apache Junction, Mesa and Tempe. (DAY TRIP 2, EAST FROM PHOENIX).

Day Trip 2

PICACHO PEAK
TUCSON

PICACHO PEAK

Tucson is an easy two-hour trip from Phoenix on I-10. Along the way, you can stop at Picacho Peak State Park, or you may wish to drive straight through and spend the entire day in Tucson.

Picacho Peak State Park. 60 miles southeast of Phoenix on I-10. This is the site of Arizona's only Civil War battle. The "Battle of Picacho" was fought here April 15, 1862. Once a landmark for Indians, as well as Butterfield Overland Mail stagecoach travelers and prospectors, this jagged mountain tells modern travelers that Tucson is near.

Two roads, the DeAnza Loop drive and the Barrett scenic loop, take you through the park. If you're in shape, hike to the top. It's a strenuous climb and not recommended from June through September. For those who want a less rugged experience, park your car and walk the trails in Picacho Peak State Park. This is an especially attractive excursion in the spring when the wildflowers are in bloom. (602) 466-3183.

TUCSON

When you think of Tucson, think mountains. The oldest continually inhabited city in the country, Tucson is surrounded by the Santa Catalinas to the north, the Rincons to the east, the Santa Rita Mountains to the south, the Tucson Mountains to the west and the Tortolita Mountains to the northwest. With an elevation of 2410 feet above sea level (about

1000 feet higher than Phoenix), the "Old Pueblo," as Tucson is called, has drier and slightly cooler climate than its big sister 100 miles to the north.

Tucson wears its Hispanic heritage like an elegant mantilla. Mexico lies just 60 miles to the south. But the Mexican influence is only one force which helped shape this city. Four cultures co-exist here: Spanish, Mexican, Native American and, of course, contemporary American.

This cultural blend adds an intellectual vitality to Tucson. Where Phoenix shines with glass and chrome, Tucson glows with pink adobe and wrought iron. Where Phoenix can be wide-open Western, Tucson can slip back in time and roll its "R's." Whether you stroll through the Barrio, the old, mostly Mexican-American neighborhood or walk the "movie-set" campus of the University of Arizona (U. of A.), you'll be acutely aware of how this half-old, half-new city pursues its blended destiny.

WHERE TO GO

Metropolitan Tucson Convention and Visitors Bureau. La Placita Village at 120 West Broadway. If you begin here, pick up additional information about the Old Pueblo. You will learn about its beginnings and how the original walled Presidio of San Agustin del Tucson was built by the Spaniards in 1776. You can see a piece of that wall preserved under glass on the second floor of the old **Pima County Courthouse** at the corner of Washington Street and Main Avenue. You'll hear about the four flags which have flown over Tucson. In 1776, the Spanish claimed it. Later, it belonged to Mexico. In 1853, Arizona was included in the Gadsden Purchase, and Tucson became part of the United States. Then, during the Civil War, the city became part of the Confederate territory.

You'll also discover some recent history and learn how Tucsonians were determined to rescue their decaying downtown. As you walk around the revitalized central city and drive through the omnipresent foothills, you'll be introduced to contemporary Tucson, a city for tomorrow.

International Business Machines (IBM) recently discovered this community and invested heavily in it after choosing Tucson over several Southwestern cities for a major plant. More recently, *Megatrends* author John Naisbitt singled out Tucson as one of the ten cities of great opportunity in the country.

As the Pima County seat, this city of about 600,000 people today serves as the economic hub for both southern Arizona and northern Mexico. As you shop and dine here, you will notice many familiar names among the commercial establishments. Several fine shops, department stores, and restaurants serve both Phoenix and Tucson. Yet in spite of the purple mountain majesty, desert climate, open skies and familiar names, you'll soon feel the difference in spirit between urban Phoenix and more laid-back Tucson, a difference which the smaller community celebrates.

WHERE TO EAT

Tucson is bursting with good places to eat. Following is just a fraction of what awaits you.

The Tack Room. 2800 Sabino Canyon Rd. Tucson's only five-star restaurant, and a local favorite for years, this definitely is worth your time and money. The continental food is excellent, the atmosphere polished and genteel. Plan an entire evening enjoying the twinkling views of Tucson in the distance, impeccable service and outstanding cuisine. $$$; □. (602) 298-2351.

Li'l Abners. 8500 N. Silverbell Rd. Li'l Abners claims it serves up "world-famous" mesquite-broiled steaks and chicken. They are delicious. This location was a Butterfield Express stage stop during pioneer days. Today it offers dining, drinking and dancing served up in a lush desert area. To get there, you'll head west on Ina Road to Silver Bell. Turn north on Silverbell. $$; □. (602) 744-2800.

Pinnacle Peak. 6541 E. Tanque Verde Rd., in Trail Dust Town. Like the Phoenix edition, this is Western living at its most casual — and dangerous if you wear a tie. Anyone who wears a tie in Pinnacle Peak risks its being cut off by the waitress or waiter in a public ceremony. The cut tie is displayed in the restaurant along with the wearer's business card. Evidently cowboys don't tolerate citified neckware. Cowboy steaks, ribs and Western pit beef in a skillet are specialties. After dinner you'll want to walk around Trail Dust Town and enjoy the shops. Even if you don't buy anything, the walk will do you good after downing a gigantic steak. $$; □. (602) 296-0911.

Carlos Murphy's. 419 W. Congress St. The specialty is 21 flavors of Margaritas; and the Mexican food is good too, at this downtown favorite. Tucsonians and tourists come for fun and crazy atmosphere. $-$$; □. (602) 628-1956.

Palomino Restaurant. 2959 N. Swan Road. Another Tucson longtime landmark, the Palomino serves excellent steaks and continental fare. $$-$$$; □. (602) 325-0413.

WHERE TO STAY

Like Phoenix, Tucson is famous for its resorts. If you have a "hankerin' " for a dude ranch, Tucson is bursting with them. There are more guest and dude ranches in Southern Arizona than anywhere else in the country. If you prefer a quick overnight in a basic motel, you can find that, too. But if you want to stay in out-of-the-ordinary accommodations, read on. Following is a sampling of special places you may want to choose. For a more complete list of accommodations, contact the Arizona Hotel & Motel Association, 3003 North Central Ave., #1204, Phoenix, AZ 85012, or call (602) 264-6081.

Tanque Verde Guest Ranch. Route 8, Box 66, Tucson. This is a Tucson landmark, a year-round ranch featuring elegant accommodations,

100 horses, tennis courts, indoor health spa, and gourmet dining. You'll need to stay longer than overnight to get a flavor of all that this ranch has to offer. Even if you don't have time on this trip, why not check Tanque Verde out for a future vacation? $$$; American Express only. (602) 296-6275.

Arizona Inn. 2200 E. Elm St. If you like historical Tucson at its most serene, you'll enjoy this world-famous hotel. There is no flash or glitz here, just unhurried, unchanged hospitality served up at its best. In the heart of town, the Arizona Inn has served an illustrious clientele over the years. Ask the staff about the celebrity guests who like the paneled, hacienda mood of this homey inn. $$$; ☐. (602) 325-1541 or (800) 421-1093.

Loews Ventana Canyon. 7000 N. Resort Dr. Tucson's most elegant addition to the total resort scene has it all. Choose from golf, tennis, swimming pools, horseback riding, nature trails, superb restaurants and health club facilities. Everything you could ask for — and more — is here in an incomparably beautiful desert setting. If you wonder how the buildings were dropped into this saguaro-studded canyon, here's the answer. During construction of the resort, these huge cacti were moved and tagged. When the buildings were completed, the original plants were replanted in the natural habitat. This not only saved the saguaros but helped to create the "we've-always-been-here" ambience. $$$; ☐. (602) 299-2020 or (800) 522-5455.

Day Trip 1

WORTH MORE TIME:
GILA BEND
YUMA

GILA BEND

Pick up this day trip following I-10 southwest out of Phoenix to its junction with I-8. Then go 62 miles west on I-8 to Gila Bend and continue 116 miles on I-10 to Yuma.

This is a long (approximately four-hour) trip, however there are enough historical attractions to make it worthwhile. If you make this trip during the hot summer months, drive during the early morning or evening hours. Along the way, you'll see the surrealistic California sand dunes near Yuma.

Gila Bend is often called the fan belt capital of the world, not because fan belts are made here, but because there are probably more belts *replaced* here than any other place in the world.

Originally, the town grew up where the Gila River took a deep bend toward the south before heading west. The community prospered when the Butterfield Overland Stage scheduled stops here in the 1870s. Miners en route to California gold fields, mail-order brides, and Eastern businessmen who were sizing up the future made themselves at home in Gila Bend for a night or two.

Then, in 1880, the train came near town, and the town gradually moved away from the river toward the tracks. Ultimately the river changed its course and moved north of town. All that's left of the river's influence is the city's name.

YUMA

Situated in the southwestern corner of the state, Yuma has an interesting heritage. History confirms that the area was visited as early as 1540 by the Spaniards. By the 1870s this community was the key southwestern city in the territory. First called Colorado City (for the river), then Arizona City (for the territory), and eventually Yuma City, the name finally was shortened to Yuma.

WHERE TO GO

Yuma Old Territorial Prison. Giss Parkway and Prison Hill Road, right off I-8 near the Colorado River. Visitors will want to see this notorious place which is now a state park. The prison operated from 1876 to 1909 and had a miserable reputation. Infamous western bad men (and women) used it as their address — folks such as Buckskin Frank Leslie and "Heartless" Pearl Hart. Exhibits feature strap-iron and granite cell blocks and describe how the prisoners lived. Open daily in the winter. Closed Tuesday and Wednesday, August through October. Fee. (602) 783-4771.

Century House Museum. 240 South Madison Ave. This was the home of pioneer merchant, E. F. Sanguinetti and is one of Yuma's oldest and most historic buildings. Now a regional museum of the Arizona Historical Society, it holds historical documents, photographs and artifacts. Walk through the gardens and aviaries on the grounds to see the birds. Open daily except Monday, and Sunday from October through April. Free. (602) 783-8020.

Quechan Indian Museum. Across the Colorado River from Yuma at Fort Yuma on Indian Hill Road, this museum is located near the territorial prison. Fort Yuma, one of the oldest military posts in Arizona, is now headquarters for the Quechan tribe. Inside you'll see exhibits of tribal artifacts. Open weekdays. Fee. (602) 572-0661.

Yuma Art Center. 281 Gila St. Located in a restored Southern Pacific Railroad depot, the center presents changing exhibitions of contemporary Arizona and Indian artists. Open Tuesday through Saturday, and on Sunday from September through mid-June. Free. (602) 783-2314.

Pick up a self-guiding tour pamphlet available at the Chamber of Commerce, 377 Main St., for more to see in Yuma. (602) 782-2567.

Day Trip 1

QUARTZSITE
PALM CANYON
PARKER
LAKE HAVASU CITY

QUARTZSITE

To visit the main destination of this day trip, Lake Havasu City, you'll drive four and one-half to five hours — one way. Obviously this trip is best done as an overnight in Lake Havasu City. Head west out of Phoenix on I-10 past Litchfield Park. Eventually, after 112 miles, I-10 intersects with A-95. Turn north on A-95 to Quartzsite.

Situated in the Mohave Desert, Quartzsite is best known for its great numbers of "snow birds" (winter visitors are called) who flock to this community each year in vast numbers pulling mobile homes with them. Visitors appreciate the sunshine and inexpensive, quiet living Quartzsite affords. The town hosts an annual rock and mineral show in February which attracts more than 850,000 people.

WHERE TO GO

Hi Jolly Monument. Quartzsite, in the Quartzsite City Cemetery. Go west on the main street from the center of town about one-fourth mile and follow the signs to the road leading to the city cemetery. Here you will see an unusual reminder of a pioneer experiment.

In the 1850s the U.S. War Department decided to introduce camels into this desert area. The Hi Jolly Monument honors Hadji Ali, one of the Arab camel drivers who was brought here to drive the beasts. The experiment was successful, but the cavalry members disliked riding the disagreeable, smelly animals. They wanted to disband the camel corps.

The official report stated that the beasts got sore feet from walking over the desert. The fact is that the cavalry got sore from riding the camels!

When the camel experiment ended, most of the other drivers went home, but Hadji Ali, or Hi Jolly as he was called, stayed to become a prospector. He is buried in the city cemetery.

Nineteen miles west of Quartzsite is Ehrenberg, a haven for rock hunters looking for agates, limonite cubes and quartz — all abundant in the area.

PALM CANYON

Hikers will want to detour south for about 20 miles on A-95 to the Kofa National Wildlife Refuge. Watch for the sign 18.7 miles south of Quartzsite which reads: "Palm Canyon and Kofa Game Range." (It's an old sign; it should say "Palm Canyon and Kofa National Wildlife Refuge!") Turn east and follow the gravel road leading to the canyon. You must drive slowly for about nine miles. There's a parking area at the end of this road. You can hike a quarter mile through the towering narrow canyon on a trail to Palm Canyon. This secluded spot, nestled in the Kofa Mountains, is home to Arizona's only native stand of palm trees.

Don't attempt to visit Palm Canyon during the hot summer months. Temperatures soar, and you'll sizzle. Hiking is at its best during the spring and autumn. The best time to visit is from the end of October through April. Open daily throughout the year. No fee. (602) 783-7861.

PARKER

Retrace your route by driving north on A-95 to its intersection with A-72. Follow A-72 northwest to Parker, which is 35 miles north of Quartzsite. If you have time to explore, stop at the Parker Chamber of Commerce, 1217 California Ave., (602) 669-2174, to pick up information. You will find a variety of events during the year, including several boat races, so check to see what's going on.

Parker is a river town — part California beach, part Arizona river rat — and exists for power and water sports. Late summer can be brutal. August temperatures climb to 120 degrees, sometimes for a week at a time.

Each year the community hosts an international innertube race in mid-June. It attracts hundreds of dedicated tubers who travel the seven miles in a variety of outlandish outfits.

WHERE TO GO

Buckskin Mountain State Park. Twenty miles north of Parker on A-95. Situated along a grassy, shady section of the riverbank, this park offers a quiet respite in often-raucous Parker. Enjoy the many campsites and hiking trails. There is a concession operation, but you might prefer to bring a picnic lunch. Open daily. Fee. (602) 667-3231.

Colorado River Indian Tribes Museum. Corner of Agency and Mohave roads in Parker. This newly-renovated museum displays the world's largest collection of Chemehuevi Indian basketry. In addition, visitors will enjoy seeing Mohave pottery and exhibits which interpret the four tribes in the area: the Mohave, Chemehuevi, Hopi and Navajo. The only museum in La Paz County, it stresses both historical and cultural exhibits. Inquire here about how to see the Blythe Intaglios, ancient Mohave figures which are etched in the nearby desert. For more information, write to the Colorado River Indian Tribes Museum, Route 1, Box 23-B, Parker, AZ 85344. Open weekdays. A donation is suggested. (602) 669-9211.

Parker Dam. On A-95 in Parker Dam, California, 17 miles north of Parker, AZ. Continue on A-95 through Parker and turn right at Agency Road. There's a stoplight. Continue on that road to the dam. As you cross the river onto the dam, you'll enter California; the Colorado River is the state boundary.

Parker Dam was built on the Colorado in 1934 and is one of the deepest dams in the world. You'll see only about one-third of the structure; the rest is under the water's surface. With a height of 320 feet and base thickness of 100 feet, it's an imposing edifice. Behind it is Lake Havasu, which contains 648,000 acre-feet of water. (An acre-foot is the amount of water it takes to cover one acre to a depth of one foot.)

You can take a self-guided tour (use 110-A) of the dam. This includes stops from the top of the dam to the generating station below the water. Taped speeches describe what you're seeing. If you've never visited a desert dam and you have a spare half hour, treat yourself to the experience and marvel at the technology. Open daily. Free. For more information, contact the Parker Chamber of Commerce in Arizona, (602) 669-2174.

LAKE HAVASU CITY

From the dam, drive north for an hour on A-95, which winds along the riverbank to Lake Havasu City. This area, like neighboring Parker, is best known for water-based recreation. You can make the Phoenix-Lake Havasu City trip in a day, but then it's more of a marathon than a day trip. It is better to plan this trip as an overnight, or even two overnights, so you have time to enjoy the area.

Lake Havasu City, established in 1963, was designed as a self-sufficient, planned community for several thousand residents. Although somewhat isolated from the rest of the state, it continues to attract newcomers and is growing into an attractive community for people who love a quiet, water-recreation life. Don't expect to see any "big city" stuff here. Come to relax, not for fine dining. Lake Havasu City is strictly small-town.

Geologically, the area around Lake Havasu and Lake Havasu City is a gold mine. Within a ten-mile radius are specimens of volcanic rock, geodes, jaspers, obsidians, turquoise and agate. Indian relics and abandoned mines also make this trip worthwhile for adventurous backpackers. If colored chips interest you more than pretty rocks, you're just 150 miles from Las Vegas and less than an hour from Laughlin, Nevada, across the Colorado River.

Make the Lake Havasu area Chamber of Commerce, 65 N. Lake Havasu Avenue, Suite 2-B, your first stop in town. As you enter Lake Havasu City, you'll come to a stoplight. Head away from the lake and drive to the top of the hill. Turn left and then take the first immediate left into the parking lot. The chamber is located in the two-story building there. Ask for a visitor's packet and dining guide. (602) 453-3444.

WHERE TO GO

Blue River Safari. Plan to take this guided boat trip while you're in Lake Havasu City to learn about the lake and the **Havasu National Wildlife Refuge,** which is located along the north shore of Lake Havasu, a few miles north of town. This wildlife preserve is home to a number of birds and small game. Fee. (602) 453-5848.

Lake Havasu and Lake Havasu State Park. This lake, which was formed when Parker Dam was built on the Colorado River, is 45 miles long and attracts fishermen, boaters, water and jet skiers, and nature lovers. To get there from town, follow London Bridge Road which sweeps along the western boundary of Lake Havasu City. As you drive, you'll see signs for many public beaches which are state-owned and operated. All types of facilities are offered — from camping to resort living.

You can rent a houseboat, jet skis or speedboat and cruise the blue lake expanse, or you can just drive to a beach, roll up your pants legs and wade around to your heart's content. The beachfront is rocky so those with tender toes should take tennis shoes.

The 13,000-acre park, which was developed along the 23 miles of shoreline surrounding Lake Havasu, contains beaches and campgrounds.

Three beaches are especially popular. **Pittsburg Point,** at Lake Havasu City, is across from the London Bridge and has a variety of concession facilities. Follow McCulloch Boulevard across the bridge and continue on McCulloch as it loops around and becomes Beachcomber Boulevard. **Windsor Beach,** north of the London Bridge on the mainland, is a good day facility and has boat-launching ramps. From

McCulloch Boulevard turn north onto London Bridge Road and go north to Windsor Beach. **Cattail Cove,** 15 miles south of Lake Havasu City on A-95, has concession campgrounds and is easily accessible to the lake. Fee. For more information, call Lake Havasu State Park. (602) 855-7851.

London Bridge. At McCulloch Boulevard and A-95, spanning Thompson Bay. Gimmicky? Of course. But there is a thrill to walking, bicycling or driving over "The" London Birdge, as incongruous as it seems suspended over the Colorado River in Arizona.

In 1967 the City of London decided that the London Bridge was too small for the current volume of traffic, so after 136 years of use, the bridge was offered for sale. Robert P. McCulloch Sr., the founder of Lake Havasu City, purchased it, had it dismantled in England with every block numbered, and shipped it to the United States. Three years later, the reconstruction was finished at a total cost of $7.5 million. It was a publicity stunt of grand proportions, and it instantly put Lake Havasu City on the map. The London Bridge formally opened in Arizona in October, 1971, to the delight of everyone who sees it.

The English Village. This is the area around the bridge which sports a full-sized village featuring gift shops and restaurants. Somehow, under the shadow of the London Bridge, it doesn't seem incongruous in its Arizona desert setting. Wander around or stop to eat at one of the restaurants or cafes.

Day Trip 1

GLENDALE
PEORIA
SUN CITIES
WICKENBURG
JOSHUA FOREST PARKWAY
GHOST TOWNS OF CONGRESS, STANTON AND OCTAVE
LAKE PLEASANT

GLENDALE

Unlike most Arizona drives, this excursion is not scenic at first. But take heart — the gorgeous desert foothills await. Along the way you'll pass through urbanizing Phoenix, visit the world's largest retirement community, and get a taste of the Old West. Be prepared for city driving plus long, open stretches. You'll cross the Agua Fria River (which may or may not have water in it depending upon the season), and view the White Tank Mountains in the distance.

Drive northwest on Grand Avenue (US-60) from Phoenix through Glendale, sometimes called "The City of Perpetual Harvest." Established in 1885 as a church community, Glendale soon became a farming town. Today it is one of the largest shipping points for fresh garden vegetables in the country. When you see roadside vendors, stop and shop. Then, continue northwest on Grand Avenue to Peoria.

PEORIA

Although not a garden spot of the Southwest, Peoria offers two attractions — especially for children.

WHERE TO GO

The Wildlife World Zoo. Three miles west of Litchfield Road on Northern Avenue. To get there, follow Grand Avenue (US-60) and turn right on Litchfield Road. At Northern Avenue, turn right again. The zoo is four miles west on Northern. Walk through an aviary with over 30 species of tropical birds, see the largest collection of marsupials (kangaroos and wallabies) in the country, all five types of the world's ostriches, and America's most complete pheasant display. Fee. (602) 935-WILD.

"A Day In The West." Follow Grand Avenue (US-60) to 99th Avenue. Turn north on 99th Avenue, then west on Carefree Highway for two miles. Follow the signs. You'll travel three miles on a gravel road to an authentic, weatherbeaten western town built by Ron Nix, a former Hollywood stuntman. You'll know you're getting close when you don't see any more telephone lines. The town is a favorite location for the movie industry, so no telephone lines infringe on the endless horizon. Nix recreated the movie set to depict the 1880s. You can visit 50 buildings on four theme streets, pan for gold, and watch live entertainment. If you're there in April, you can see the Stuntman's Rodeo. Fee for adults only. Children free. (602) 866-7698.

WHERE TO EAT

"A Day In The West." A steak fry is staged here each Saturday night. Miss Kitty's saloon has cold drinks and snacks. Call in advance for reservations. $-$$; no cards. (602) 866-7698.

SUN CITIES

Back on Grand Avenue (US-60) continue northwest through Youngtown to Del Webb's Sun City and Sun City West. These retirement cities are about 20 miles from downtown Phoenix. You'll know you're near when you see more electric golf carts than cars on the streets! Established in 1954, Youngtown was the first retirement community in the United States and continues to attract retirees. However, that town has been eclipsed in size by the Del Webb developments which were begun in 1960. Today Sun City and Sun City West comprise the world's largest retirement communities. Even if you aren't thinking of giving up the office for golf, they are worth a visit.

At Sun City West, your driving tour includes Sundome Plaza, the vast Sundome Center for the Performing Arts, sports pavilion, Johnson Library and other points of interest. For information, call (602) 975-2270, or visit the development office, 13323 Meeker Blvd.

WICKENBURG

Leaving the golf-cart set behind, follow A-93 north to Wickenburg for a taste of the old and the new West. As you proceed, you'll enter rolling foothills dotted with saguaros, ocotillos and mesquite.

Wickenburg is located approximately 54 miles northwest of Phoenix and sits at the foot of the Bradshaw Mountains on the banks of the Hassayampa (Hah-sa-yampa) River. Legend has it that anyone who drinks from the Hassayampa never tells the truth again. As you approach the Hassayampa you may wonder how anyone ever drinks out of the river anyway, since usually it is a wide, dry, sandy riverbed. But look again. The green, lush area around it demonstrates the power of a desert river. Even a sporadic flow of water creates fertile soil out of dusty ground.

Wickenburg was established by Henry Wickenburg who searched for an elusive vein of gold for ten years. There are numerous stories about how he finally found gold. Some may be more truthful, but this legend is the best: When the failed prospector landed in what is now called Wickenburg, he was discouraged and alone. His partner had no faith in him, and, to make matters worse, Wickenburg had a bulky burro which refused to move. Looking up, the prospector saw a vulture circle, land and eye the stubborn beast. In utter disgust, Wickenburg picked up a rock to throw at the bird. When the rock dropped, it split in half and revealed gold.

Regardless of the veracity of that tale, Wickenburg inadvertently stumbled over the richest gold lode in Arizona. He named it the Vulture Mine. Although his claim has long been exhausted and is no longer even open for tours, the town of Wickenburg retains its rustic gold rush image.

WHERE TO GO

Frontier Street. This area is preserved as it was in the 1800s with a fine railway station, a former hotel and other buildings. Follow US-60 west as it crosses the Hassayampa River. Frontier intersects with US-60. Wander at will.

Desert Caballeros Western Museum. 20 N. Frontier St. Turn left onto Frontier from US-60. Parking is next to the railroad tracks. Staffed and built by dedicated volunteers, this museum contains works by well-known Western artists, including Frederic Remington and George Phippen. In addition to the art gallery, visit the Hall of History, period rooms, mineral room and Mexican room. Fee for adults. (602) 684-2272.

Old 761. At Apache and Tegner streets behind the Town Hall. From the museum, follow Frontier Street northwest to Apache Street. Turn right on Apache to just north of Tegner Street. Here you will see the original steam engine and tender that chugged along the track from Chicago to the West.

Jail Tree. Tegner and Center streets. From Old 761, follow Apache Street south. Turn left onto Tegner Street. You'll come upon a large, 200-year-old mesquite tree. Since Wickenburg didn't have a jail, the law used this tree to tether rowdies who caused trouble. You can see the leg irons, still attached to the tree, which accomplished the task. Law-abiding citizens can stop, clamp on the irons, and have their pictures taken.

WHERE TO EAT

The Wickenburg Inn Tennis & Guest Ranch. Prescott Highway, seven miles northwest of Wickenburg on US-89. Not gourmet, but reasonable and pleasant. Come for good American fare — chicken, fish, and steaks. Reservations suggested. $$; □. (602) 684-7811.

Rancho de los Caballeros. Five miles west of Wickenburg and two miles south of US-60 on Vulture Mine Road. A little more expensive, but you can count on finding an assortment of hearty Western favorites such as chicken, fish and steaks. Reservations suggested. Open late fall to early spring. $$; no cards. (602) 684-5484.

JOSHUA FOREST PARKWAY

Northwest on US-93, 20 miles beyond Wickenburg, you'll be greeted by one of nature's more unusual welcoming committees: a strange, dense forest of Joshua trees. Located on both sides of the highway, hordes of thick-trunked cactus crowd the landscape and mesmerize passing tourists.

Joshua trees, which are actually tall, bristly yucca plants, were named by Mormon pioneers who thought the upright branches pointed toward the Promised Land. These slow-growing trees provide homes for 25 species of birds. In addition, packrats gnaw off spiny leaf blades, and night lizards find that the rotted-out bark of wind-toppled Joshua trees provides their entire world. Usually found in the Mohave Desert, Joshua trees rarely are found in the Sonoran Desert, which makes this dense stand all the more exciting.

GHOST TOWNS OF CONGRESS STANTON AND OCTAVE

You may return to Phoenix from Wickenburg by heading southeast on US-89/A-93. Or, if you are up for adventure and have adequate gas in the tank, follow US-89 north 16 miles on a paved road to Congress for a leisurely journey through some authentic ghost towns. In Arizona, "authentic" means that you won't find snack bars, concession stands or gift shops. What you *will* find are the ghosts of buildings from Arizona's past — crumbling structures slowly dying in the desert. Consequently, before you turn off onto the back road leading to Congress, Stanton and Octave, if you see facilities and need to stop, do so.

You may prefer to combine this excursion with your return trip on US-89 south from Yarnell and Peeples Valley (SEE DAY TRIP 2, NORTH FROM PHOENIX).

Started as a mining camp, Congress was established in 1887. By 1891, it was estimated that $600,000 was shipped from that mine, although it's possible that more than $1 million actually was taken out. After 1919, mining activity slowed to a trickle and the town faded away. As you drive on this paved road, known only as "the road to Congress," look around. You'll see crumbling foundations and faded memories of a once-glorious past. Only the dump of the mine stands within sight of the present town of Congress Junction.

Continue through Congress Junction about four miles and then turn right onto a gravel road. Watch for the sign that says that this is the road to Stanton and follow it. It looks rough, but it is graded and passable for passenger cars. Stanton is about seven miles from Congress. As you bump along the road to this ghost town, note that it was built by pioneer C. C. Genung in 1871 at a cost of $7650. Genung paid white men $75 a month, Mexicans received $65 a month, and Indians got 50 cents a day plus beans, flour, sugar, coffee and venison. Today Stanton is privately owned.

When you reach Stanton, you'll want to investigate what's left of this mining camp. Originally called Antelope Station, the town was located on an old stage route and renamed for Charles P. Stanton, who was deputy county recorder. Legend has it that Stanton was a defrocked priest. For sure, he was a man of doubtful character. He ran the town, and he and the "Stanton Gang" raked in gold at the expense of the community. It's rumored that his gang cost Arizona settlers "more than all the Apaches put together." Ultimately Charles Stanton met his demise when he was shot by a man who believed that Stanton had insulted his sister.

Travel a few more miles on this same road to reach Octave, which is located 13 miles from Wickenburg. Now a maze of stone foundations, cellar pits and ruins, it was once a bustling town of 3000 hardy souls who came here for gold in 1863. Eventually $8 million was taken out of the quartz veins of Octave Mine. The mine continued in operation until World War II. Today it belongs to the wind, sun and sand and to those adventurous types who love the silent, brooding allure of ghost towns.

As is true of any of Arizona's back roads, don't attempt to navigate the road to Stanton during rainy weather. The slick mountains and barren desert make flash floods a real hazard. (See the section on FLASH FLOODS at the end of this book.)

LAKE PLEASANT

To complete your day, what better excursion than to get out of the dusty ghost towns and head for Lake Pleasant. To reach this recreation site, go southeast on US-89 and backtrack for about 11 miles. At the junction of US-89 and A-74, follow A-74 east to Lake Pleasant, one of the many man-made lakes dotting the Arizona desert. Arizonans take water seriously — damming rivers for flood control, surface water and recreation. You may be surprised to know that Arizona has one of the highest boats-per-capita ratios in the country.

Lake Pleasant was formed when Waddell Dam was constructed on the Agua Fria River. Picnic, rent jet skis or just enjoy the rocky landscape and cool views before returning to Phoenix. When you're ready to end your day, travel east on A-74 to I-17. Follow I-17 south to Phoenix. Or back track west on A-74 and pick up A-93 southeast to Phoenix.

Day Trips
From Tucson

Welcome to Southern Arizona. With Tucson as your base, you can roam back roads, poke around ghost towns, or ascend Kitt Peak to view some of the world's most sophisticated optical instruments. You'll find everything here, from quaint historical settings to a gleaming, growing city. Because Southern Arizona encompasses such a vast area, you may wonder how you're going to see it all if you're not familiar with the territory. Relax. As you read through the suggested trips, you'll quickly understand the logical progression described. Several of the day excursions link up easily with each other creating pleasant opportunities for overnight vacations.

Historically, agriculture and copper mining served as the basis for the economy in this part of the state. However, tourism quickly is becoming the most important industry. You'll discover, as you travel through this region, that even the smallest towns offer clean, comfortable facilities for visitors.

Before you set off, examine your road map. You'll see that the land in southern Arizona is owned by a number of different entities. Most of the countryside belongs to Yuma, Pima, Cochise, Pinal and Graham counties, but the area also includes several national monuments, wildlife preserves, national forests and Indian reservations, the largest of which is the Papago (pronounced Pop'-a-go) west of Tucson. In Arizona, driving in and out of reservations is like crossing different counties. You won't notice much difference except, possibly, a change in the surface of the road.

You'll also see, if you look closely, that two areas are labeled "Saguaro National Monument." This isn't a mistake. The larger one lies due east of Tucson; the smaller portion of the park is located west of the city, and both are referred to as "Saguaro National Monument."

Although southern Arizona is located south of Phoenix, the elevation around Tucson is higher than that of the capital city. You drive "down" to Tucson, but are actually driving "up." Be prepared for *slightly* cooler and drier temperatures in the immediate vicinity of the Old Pueblo.

You may want to refer to DAY TRIP 2, SOUTHEAST FROM PHOENIX to brush up on what's available in Tucson before reading this portion of the book.

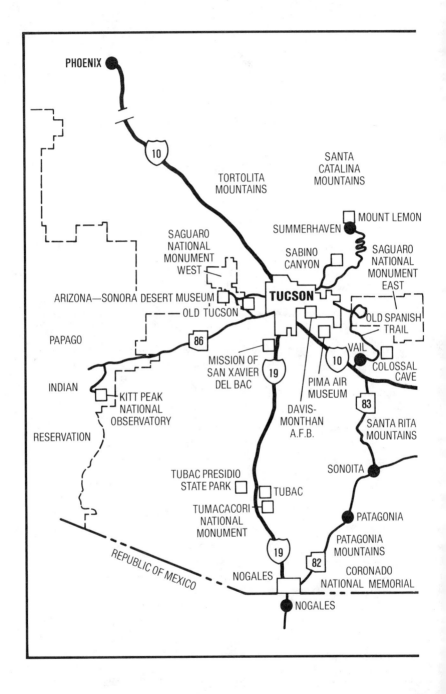

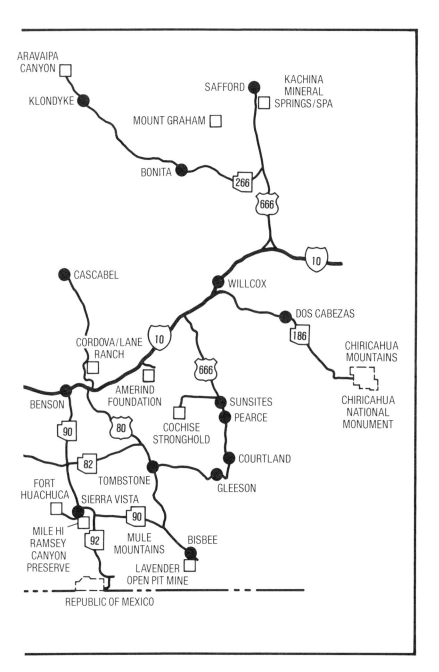

ARAVAIPA CANYON

KLONDYKE

SAFFORD

KACHINA MINERAL SPRINGS/SPA

MOUNT GRAHAM

BONITA

266

666

10

CASCABEL

WILLCOX

DOS CABEZAS

186

CHIRICAHUA MOUNTAINS

CORDOVA/LANE RANCH

10

666

CHIRICAHUA NATIONAL MONUMENT

BENSON

AMERIND FOUNDATION

SUNSITES

PEARCE

90

80

COCHISE STRONGHOLD

82

COURTLAND

FORT HUACHUCA

TOMBSTONE

GLEESON

SIERRA VISTA

90

MILE HI RAMSEY CANYON PRESERVE

92

MULE MOUNTAINS

BISBEE

LAVENDER OPEN PIT MINE

REPUBLIC OF MEXICO

Day Trip 1

SABINO CANYON
MOUNT LEMMON

SABINO CANYON

Prepare for a day in the great outdoors. You'll begin your drive in Tucson, surrounded by the urban scene. But as you head out toward the Santa Catalina Mountains, you'll quickly leave the city behind. One of the beauties of this day trip is that you can enjoy some of the area's most magnificent wilderness so close to home. To do both areas justice in one day, you'll need to leave early and not linger too long at either. This could be a problem because both Sabino Canyon and Mount Lemmon have endless trails to hike and acres of serenity to enjoy.

Although this day trip stars Mother Nature at her finest, she is fickle. Take an extra wrap along. Depending upon the season, carry a windbreaker, heavy sweater or even a ski jacket in the car. As you climb to the summit of Mount Lemmon, you'll experience a major change in climate. You also need comfortable walking shoes. Although primarily an unspoiled area, there are easy trails and nearby amenities.

If you plan to drive to the top of Mount Lemmon during the winter months, it's wise to call ahead to check on the weather. If it's cloudy or rainy in Tucson, it could be snowing at the summit. Although the road to Mount Lemmon is paved, snow can make it impassable. Even the most adventurous types wouldn't get caught without chains or a four-wheel-drive vehicle.

New York City has Central Park, but Tucson has Sabino Canyon, a woodsy respite close to town. Nestled in the foothills of the Santa Catalina Mountains, Sabino Canyon is a hiker's, picnicker's and lovers' dream. With its streams and waterfalls, hiking and biking trails, this natural area manages to absorb the horde of visitors who turn to it every day for a needed dose of calm and quiet.

To get there, follow Wilmot Road north to where it joins with Tanque Verde Road. Head northeast on Tanque Verde and across the Pantano Wash to its intersection with Sabino Canyon Road which takes you to the visitors center. You must park your car here and proceed either on foot or by bus for the four-mile trip to the first of several recreation areas. The tram runs frequently and there are regular moonlight rides offered from March through December. Fee. (602) 749-2861.

WHERE TO GO

Pick up a trail map at the visitors center. Then as you walk along, you may observe the different kinds of trees growing here. Pine and fir forest the slopes about the streambed. Deep within the canyon, you'll find other trees, including willow, box elder and alder. In the lower elevations, Sabino is host to cactus, paloverde and even saguaros, while along the streambed, you'll find shady sycamore, cottonwood, ash and walnut trees.

Why the name Sabino?" No one is exactly sure. One school of thought insists that the name comes from a plant called "sabino" or "savino." The more accepted story is that it was named for a Mexican rancher who lived in the area in the 1870s. Regardless of its history, Sabino Canyon has established itself as Tucson's glorious canyon-in-residence, an ideal getaway in every season.

The tram was installed to help preserve the air quality and environment. Along the way it stops at designated observation sites. During the winter months, moonlight excursions offer a totally different experience. If you've never taken a guided tour in a national park at night or seen a wild area after sunset, you should do this. Tickets are available next to the visitors center parking area. For more information contact Sabino Canyon Shuttle, Route 15, Box 280, Tucson, AZ 85715, or call (602) 749-2861.

MOUNT LEMMON

To get to Mount Lemmon from Sabino Canyon, follow Sabino Canyon Road south to Tanque Verde Road. Turn east on Tanque Verde to Catalina Highway. Follow Catalina Highway northeast to Mount Lemmon. This is an extremely popular area and is well marked. Just watch for signs to Mount Lemmon.

As you drive along Tanque Verde toward Catalina Highway, you will see some elegant residential areas. Tucson is famous for its low-slung, hacienda-type homes and bright blue pools hidden among the saguaros and ocotillos.

Catalina Highway, also called the road to Mount Lemmon, climbs the mountain's southern slope. From this point, the 30-mile drive will take about an hour up the 9157-foot mountain. Although the road is perfectly safe for automobile traffic, those who can't look down from a tall building may not enjoy this experience. Queasy passengers who still want a view should just look up.

As you head up this queen peak of the Santa Catalinas, you'll pass scenic viewpoints and see areas marked for camping and picnicking. You can even stop and fish; signs will lead you to a lake stocked with trout. Along the way you'll get a graphic lession in physical geography. Even if you've never taken a course in this subject and know nothing about it, you cannot help but learn something on this trip. Your drive will take you through five distinct life zones — areas which support specific types of vegetation. You'll begin with the Sonoran desert and climb through piñon and juniper to pine. Soon you'll be into elevations supporting fir trees and, eventually, aspen trees. This is the same vegetation change you would observe were you to drive from Arizona to the Canadian border. Not surprisingly, the drive is gorgeous in autumn and spring.

Once at the top, hike around. If you've packed a picnic lunch, this is the place to spread it out and relax. Enjoy the crisp cool air and the views which stretch forever. Remember, while perched in this northern clime, that you are just one hour — and some 7000 feet — away from the desert floor.

WHERE TO GO

Summerhaven. At the summit of Mount Lemmon. Spend some time walking around this friendly mountaintop hamlet. There's an entire community up here, including a lodge offering rustic accommodations, small cabins, campgrounds and other amenities. You can eat, use the restrooms and fill the car with gas. Because you're at the top of a 9100 plus-foot mountain, don't expect too much luxury and you'll be pleasantly surprised by the charm. (602) 576-1400.

Mount Lemmon Ski Lift. In the winter, if the snow is right, Mount Lemmon becomes the southernmost ski area in the United States. In the summer, ride the lift for the breathtaking view. The 25-minute round trip covers approximately one mile. You'll depart near the base area and look over the San Pedro Valley, the Reef of Rocks and the towns of Oracle and Mammoth. Fee. (602) 576-1400.

WHERE TO EAT

Iron Door Restaurant. In Ski Valley, at the base of the Mount Lemmon ski area. Come for salads, sandwiches, homemade soups, skiers chili and cornbread. The restaurant is named for a lost mine with an iron door which, legend has it, was operated by Jesuit padres in the Catalinas during the 1700s. According to the story, Apache raiders killed the Papago mine workers and the Jesuits. Lunch only. $$; no cards. (602) 576-1400.

To return to Tucson, retrace your steps down the mountain and follow Tanque Verde Road back into town.

Day Trip 1

DAVIS-MONTHAN AIR FORCE BASE
SAGUARO NATIONAL MONUMENT (EAST)
COLOSSAL CAVE

DAVIS MONTHAN AIR FORCE BASE

It's difficult to imagine that this immense base started as a municipal airport established by civic-minded citizens in 1919. Located on Craycroft Road at Golf Links Road in Tucson, Davis-Monthan is named for Lts. Samuel H. Davis and Oscar Monthan, two early Air Corps officers from Tucson.

The Army Air Corps made its first investment in D-M in 1931, and modern paved roads and runways followed in the mid-30s. Shortly before Pearl Harbor, $3 million was earmarked for expansion, and D-M soon became one of the best heavy bombardment training stations in the nation.

After World War II, the base was nearly deserted until it was designated an Air Technical Service Command storage area. Because of the arid climate, hundreds of aircraft are stored here now.

Currently D-M is a diversified military installation. It is home to the largest outdoor aircraft storage facility in the world, and A-10 combat crew training and OA-37 Forward Air Control operations also are conducted. With all the fighter planes and helicopters constantly in the air, the skies over D-M are rarely quiet.

WHERE TO GO

Base Tours. Craycroft and Golf Links Roads. Tours are available each Monday and Wednesday morning. Longer photographic tours are offered the second Saturday of each month. A base bus picks up visitors at the front gate of the base on South Craycroft Road near the intersection of Golf Links. Free. For additional information, write to Headquarters, 836th Air Division, Public Affairs; Attn: Community Relations, Davis-Monthan AFB, AZ 85707 or call (602) 748-3204 or 748-3091.

Pima Air Museum. 6400 S. Wilmot Rd. To get to this privately operated museum from Davis-Monthan, take Craycroft north to 22nd Street. Turn west to Alvernon Rd., then go south to I-10 and take I-10 west to the Wilmot Road exit, number 269. Turn north on Wilmot and continue for two miles. Wilmot Road dead ends, and the museum is right there.

Although not technically part of Davis-Monthan, the facility works closely with the base. The third largest air museum in the country, it is exceeded in size only by the Smithsonian Institution's National Air and Space Museum in Washington, D.C., and the Wright-Patterson Air Museum in Dayton, Ohio. More than 130 civilian, military and historical planes are displayed at the Pima Air Museum. Ask if a special volunteer is available to take you through the presidential aircraft located on the grounds.

Snacks and soft drinks may be purchased at the museum which is open every day except Christmas. Fee. (602) 574-0462.

SAGUARO NATIONAL MONUMENT

As you look at your map of this area, note that the Saguaro National Monument is actually two parks. The larger one, the Rincon Mountain Section unit, is located due east of Tucson, while the smaller park, the Tucson Mountain District unit, lies to the west. Both parks were established March 1, 1933, for the protection of a remarkable stand of saguaro (pronounced "swar-o") cactus found here. Thanks to excellent management they offer desert travelers a treat for the eyes. Note that there are no accomodations available other than picnic tables at either of these facilities.

Return to I-10 when you leave the Pima Air Museum. Go east on I-10 to exit 275 and continue north on this road to Old Spanish Trail. Turn east on Old Spanish Trail for two miles to the entrance of **Saguaro National Monument East** or Rincon Mountain Section Unit. Take the nine-mile Cactus Forest Drive loop to the visitors center. It's open from 7 a.m. to sunset.

Driving through a stand of saguaros is unlike driving through any other kind of forest. The profusion of angles will constantly delight you. Some saguaros signal with their arms in crazy directions; others stand almost perfectly symmetrical with arms reaching up in supplication. Although a stately plant, saguaros nevertheless strike some humorous poses.

As you walk or drive through the 62,499 acres of this section of Saguaro National Monument, you'll be amazed at the endless variety and sheer numbers of the plants. The visitors center has information on the native vegetation, and you'll get an overview of the biology and geology found in this area of the state. Hopefully you'll come away with a better understanding of how plants and animals adapt to an arid existence. Above all, you'll gain a new appreciation for that wondrous plant, the saguaro.

The saguaro cactus is remarkable. A natural desert condominium, it provides homes for a variety of creatures. Several species of birds eat its seeds, live in its walls and build nests in its arms. By the time a saguaro grows to 20 feet and has its first branch, the plant has lived through 75 years of strenuous desert sun, wind and rain. With a root structure stretching for miles and miles just barely beneath the surface, the plant is an unparalleled natural balancing act. Superbly adapted to make the most of an unpredictable desert water supply, the plant's accordion-style pleats allow it to shrink during droughts and plump up after rains. Given optimum conditions, secure from bulldozers and development, this queen of the desert can grow to 50 feet and survive to age 200.

Birdwatchers will have a field day at Saguaro National Monument. More than 50 species of reptiles also roam the park. If you've thought of the desert as an empty place, think again. As you wander this rolling saguaro-studded landscape with its endless shades of sun-bleached green, look for desert tortoises, gophers, coach-whip snakes, ground squirrels, peccaries, coyotes and mule deer. Listen, too, for the whistle of the curve-bill thrasher, the churring of the cactus wren and a yipping coyote chorus.

Take a stroll down one of the more gentle nature trails mentioned in a free, self-guided pamphlet you can pick up at the visitors center. If you visit between February and May, you may be fortunate enough to witness an outstanding wildflower display. These fragile blooms are dependent upon winter rain, so a superb show is not guaranteed each year. If you're there when these blossoms peak, you're in for a special desert experience.

Outdoor types may prefer hiking in the forests of the Rincon Mountains. A backpacking permit is required in the backcountry. Contact the National Park Service, Saguaro National Monument, Rt. 8, Box 695, Tucson, AZ 85730 for more details. The visitors center is open daily. Free. (602) 296-8576.

COLOSSAL CAVE

As you leave Saguaro National Monument, continue south on Old Spanish Trail for ten more miles. You'll see the signs for Colossal Cave, an underground wilderness experience.

Just 22 miles from Tucson, the rocky entrance to this cave has been compared to a Tibetan monastery. Inside, a myriad of winding rooms leads to still-unexplored vistas. Colossal Cave is the largest dry cavern in the world and although explorers have been at it for years, they have yet to find its end. The names of the rooms describe the wonders — crystal halls, cathedral room, the bandits' campground and kingdom of the elves.

Regardless of the weather, Colossal Cave remains a comfortable 72 degrees year-round. Frequent guided tours ferry visitors through the cavern. Colossal Cave is open daily including Sundays and holidays. Fee. (602) 791-7677.

To return to Tucson, continue on Old Spanish Trail from Colossal Cave to Vail. At Vail, pick up I-10 (A-86) northwest and continue into Tucson. Or you can head east on I-10 to Day Trip 2 of this sector.

Day Trip 2

BENSON
WILLCOX AND THE COCHISE STRONGHOLD
GHOST TOWNS OF COCHISE COUNTY

BENSON

Follow I-10 east to Benson, about 45 miles from Tucson. This small community, like its neighbor Willcox, was founded along the main line of the Southern Pacific Railroad. During the late 1800s it served as a shipping point for the livestock- and mineral-producing areas to the south. It nestles into an intermountain valley created by the San Pedro River. Although the original streets were designed in a grid on a 160-acre plat, the town grew haphazardly.

Today Benson is emerging as a suburb of Tucson. Surrounded by natural beauty, the immediate area offers a wealth of things to see and do.

WHERE TO GO

Amerind Foundation. Exit 318, south of I-10 in Texas Canyon between Benson and Willcox. Take the Triangle-T — Dragoon exit (318) on I-10 and continue east one mile to the Amerind Foundation turnoff. Turn left at the sign: FF Ranch-Amerind.

This museum is a jewel. A privately-funded center for archeological field research, the center also houses a museum and art gallery dedicated to archeological and ethnographical material on Indians from all the Americas. The gallery contains a superb collection of Western, Indian and American art.

Why a fine museum in the middle of the desert? The answer lies in the passions of one man, William Shirley Fulton, a Connecticut industrialist. Fulton purchased this property, 65 miles east of Tucson, in the early 1930s and became intensely involved in Native American cultures. As he began to acquire a sizeable collection of diverse artifacts, Fulton hired noted architect H. M. Starkweather to design and build a permanent home for his important collection. Starkweather visualized the Spanish Colonial Revival Style structure as an eloquent contrast to the massive natural boulders of this part of Arizona.

Until recently the Amerind Foundation (the name refers to the prehistoric Indians who lived in the Americas) concentrated more on research than outreach. Now the Amerind has redirected its focus and is making its impressive collection of artifacts, arts and crafts more accessible to visitors. Open daily. Fee. (602) 586-3003.

WHERE TO STAY

Cordova/Lane Ranch. From Benson, continue east on I-10 to exit 306. Follow that road toward Cascabel. When the hardtop pavement ends, continue one and one-third miles on the dirt road. You'll see a sign on the right to this guest ranch.

If you are up to seeing the country the way it is meant to be seen — from atop a horse — pay a visit to Cordova/Lane Ranch which is especially marvelous during the spring and fall months. The ranch staff asks just 24 hours' advance notice.

There is no better way to see the rugged Cochise County countryside than on horseback. Guided horse tours can last a few hours or overnight. A breakfast ride and an all-day trip to Gammons Gulch, an authentic Western movie set, are available. A wonderful family excursion is the ride to Fort Bowie on the actual Butterfield Stage route into the fort where Geronimo was held. The American flag fluttering over the ruins of the fort is an impressive patriotic display. More adventurous travelers may enjoy a full day or overnight ride into Cochise Stronghold, where the Apaches held off the American Army for an incredible eight years in the late 1800s. For more information, write to Cordova/Lane Ranch: L. Cordova or Bud Lane, P. O. Box 433, Pomerene, AZ 85627. Fee. (602) 586-2066.

WILLCOX

From Benson, follow I-10 east 36 miles to Willcox. This small Arizona community was settled in 1880 as a construction camp for the Southern Pacific Railroad. When the track went down, Willcox sprang to life. It quickly became a focal point in Cochise County for cattle shipping a still holds that position. Some of the largest cattle ranches in the sta . are located in the broad, grassy valleys in the area.

Often called the "Gateway to the Chiricahua Wonderland," Willcox is rich with Indian lore. Here the United States Calvary battled the Chiricahua Apaches. Many sites commemorate various skirmishes. This is the country of Cochise, the legendary Apache chief who stalked and struck deep in the valleys and then faded back into the shadowy mountains. This land was holy to all Apaches. The Apache chief Geronimo wrote: "There is no place equal to that of Arizona. I want to spend my last days there and be buried among those mountains."

Today Willcox is known as the home of television, movie and radio personality Rex Allen. But if ghosts intrigue you more than cowboys, you'll want to see the wonderful old ghost towns and graveyards in this vicinity. At one time these towns were mining camps full of fights and brawls. Today they lie silently under the Arizona sun. If you pay a visit to the Old Willcox Cemetery, southeast of town, you'll see where Warren Earp, brother of the famous frontier marshall, Wyatt Earp, is buried. For more information about the ghost towns in the area and other points of interest, drop by the Willcox Chamber of Commerce, 1500 North Circle I Road. (602) 384-2272.

WHERE TO GO

The Cochise Information Center and Museum of the Southwest. 1500 North Circle I Road, Willcox. Stop here for information about this area and tour the museum. When you enter, you'll be greeted with an impressive bust of Cochise. Take the time to read some of his sayings recorded here, and you'll get an insight into the mind of this unusual man. You may also want to stroll around Heritage Park on the grounds of the center where you'll see a replica of an Indian village, a nature trail and a mining display. (602) 384-2272.

Cochise Stronghold. Follow I-10 west about eight miles from Willcox. Take US-666 south about 17 miles. About a mile before you get to the community of Sunsites, there is an unnamed graded road heading west. Look for the sign indicating that this is the road to Cochise Stronghold. Take this road west for ten miles until it ends at the parking lot and campgrounds.

Cochise Stronghold is the area of the Dragoon Mountains which served as home, headquarters and safe haven for Apache Chief Cochise. Cochise was a fierce leader, on a par with Geronimo and Mangas Coloradas. As you drive into the mountains here, more than one writer has noted a "presence" which seems to linger over the landscape. Somewhere in this tangle of rocks and canyons, towers and domes, and manzanita shrubs lie the bones of Cochise. Even in death, he remains a controversial character.

One legend says that when Cochise died in 1874, his braves buried him in full regalia. They lowered his body into a deep crevice along with his horse, dog and rifle. According to another story, his men, fearing vandalism by white men, buried their chief on a grassy mesa and then ran their horses back and forth to mask the grave site. In any event, although the exact location of Cochise's body is unknown, his spirit is everywhere.

As you enter the area of the Stronghold, you'll see a Forest Service campground. A good hiking trail into the Dragoon Mountains begins here. If you decide to explore this region, remember that the area is not commercially developed. You won't find any souvenir shops or cafes at the end of your journey which takes about four hours. If you're prepared for a rugged walk, park at the campground and follow the well-marked three-mile trail. Some of the climb is steep, but eventually you'll arrive at an open area where you can gaze over a 40-mile vista. This point on the trail is designated as the heart of the Stronghold. As you stand there, surrounded by the cliffs and sculpted spires, it's easy to imagine Apache bands moving in and out of the shadows.

When you start down, you'll need to watch your footing because the path is steep. Around the two-mile mark, turn to see towering above the walnut and sycamore trees an almost overpowering view of Cochise Stonghold. It's the same scene that greeted Gen. O. O. Howard as he marched into the Stronghold in 1872 carrying a flag of truce. As a result of Howard's trek, Cochise agreed to end the hostilities at last.

No doubt General Howard had other things on his mind than the scenery. But, as you leave the Stronghold, take one last, lingering look at this Apache sanctum. Don't be surprised if you have the distinct feeling that the great Chief Cochise is looking back at you.

A word of caution. This area has no amenities other than picnic tables — not even a telephone.

GHOST TOWNS OF COCHISE COUNTY

To do the ghost towns justice, plan on a full day of touring. It's tough to rush ghosts. The entire area — bounded by Sierra Vista, Benson and Willcox to the north and the Mexican border to the south — is a ghost-town hunter's dream. During the mining boom, this countryside was thick with camps and communities that sprang up with a shout and died out with a whimper when the ore disappeared.

Today visitors can stand among the crumbling rubble and easily imagine wild-eyed young men and sassy young women who lived here drunk on the easy money. Even if you don't believe in spirits, ghost towns have a calming effect which infects the most skeptical tourist. As you stand looking at the whisps of streets, pieces of foundation, and crooked walls that defy gravity, you cannot help but hear the whispers of past action.

Each of these communities once burst with activity. They were crowded with saloons and stores and homes, as long as the gold, silver and copper came in, so did the men hunting quick fortunes and fast women. Now, although the music has stopped, the energy lingers.

If you visit during the summer months, bring a jug of water and wear a hat so that you don't fade too fast. As you visit the ghost towns, you'll find that at least two communities, Dos Cabezas (DAY TRIP 3, EAST OF TUCSON) and Pearce, have refused to give up the ghost completely. Real-live people reside in these communities and you'll even find food and drink at Pearce.

WHERE TO GO

Pearce. From Cochise Stronghold, retrace your route and head east on the graded road to Arizona Sunsites, a new community catering to both the family and retirement crowd. One and a half miles south of Sunsites, on your right, is the road to Old Pearce. This is where Ghost Town Trail begins. Follow the signs directing you to the Old General Store.

The Commonwealth Mine put Pearce on the map around 1890 when Johnny Pearce struck gold. More gold came from this mine than from any other mine in the territory. At Pearce you can visit the old cemetery, which is still used today. Abraham Lincoln's bodyguard is buried here as are some Union and Confederate soldiers and a few of Pearce's "tarnished belles" from its more lively era. The Old General Store and museum are full of Old West items which visitors enjoy poking through.

WHERE TO EAT

Cochise Adobe Inn. US-666 and High Street at the entrance to Sunsites. Here you'll find a real surprise — leisurely dining and home cooked food in the middle of Ghost Town Trail. Seafood is a specialty. The desserts are homemade without preservatives. Open daily for breakfast, lunch and dinner. $$; □. (602) 826-3886.

WANDERING THE BACKROADS

To visit more ghost towns, continue south on the road past Pearce. It winds through the old mining towns of Courtland and Gleeson ending up at Tombstone, where you can connect to DAY TRIP 1, SOUTHEAST OF TUCSON.

Courtland. On Ghost Town Trail to Tombstone. There's one resident in Courtland and he does not encourage visitors. As you drive by, you may want to take a passing glance at this once-thriving mining camp.

If you decide to explore on foot, don't expect to be greeted by any famous Southwestern hospitality.

Gleeson. On Ghost Town Trail 16 miles east of Tombstone. Turquoise put Gleeson on the map. Even before the Spaniards arrived, the Indians in the area mined this stone. Later residents found zinc, copper and lead. Modern visitors will find picturesque ruins to wander through and a cemetery to explore.

To get a complete listing on Arizona ghost towns, write to the Arizona Office of Tourism, 1480 E. Bethany Home Rd., Phoenix, AZ 85014. (602) 255-3618. You can spend a day or two exploring the old towns in this region of the state. If you have time, pick up a book on Arizona history. The more you know, the more you'll appreciate what you're seeing.

After Gleeson, you have a choice. Continue to Tombstone (see DAY TRIP 1, SOUTHEAST OF TUCSON) and stay overnight there or go through Tombstone, heading north on US 80 to I-10, and following I-10 west to Tucson.

Day Trip 3

CHIRICAHUA NATIONAL MONUMENT
DOS CABEZAS

CHIRICAHUA NATIONAL MONUMENT

From Tucson follow I-10 east to Willcox. At the junction of A-186, turn south and follow this road about 20 miles to the Chiricahua National Monument. If you pick up this trip at Safford, take US-666 south to I-10, head west to A-186 and follow it to the park. After paying the entrance fee proceed to the visitors center. The exhibits here graphically describe both the man-made and natural history of this mountainous area. You may pick up pamphlets or buy guide books describing the various trails. If you take the time to go through the visitors center first, you'll appreciate this region of the country much more.

Described as "a wonderland of balanced rocks, volcanic spires and grotesquely eroded cliffs," Chiricahua National Monument was established in 1924. Endlessly mysterious, this is an ever-changing landscape. One moment shadows caress the spires that rise nearly 200 feet into the air; the next, light plays hide-and-seek with chiseled rocks that stand silently shoulder to shoulder.

Plan this day trip when you have lots of time and energy. If you want advance information, contact the Chiricahua National Monument, Dos Cabezas Star Route, Willcox, AZ 85643. (602) 824-3560.

WHAT TO DO

To see this sprawling park from the comfort of your car, follow Massai Point Drive, a six and one-half mile paved road that leads up Bonita

Canyon to Massai Point. From the top you'll get a good view of Sulphur Springs Valley to the west and San Simon Valley to the east. The Massai Point Exhibit Building is a worthwhile stop for it offers more information on the natural history of the area.

However, you'll experience the sense of the Chiricahuas more if you travel on foot. There are over 17 miles of trails to choose from. If you plan to hike for more than an hour, take water with you. Whether you decide on a 20-minute stroll or a two-and-a-half hour hike, you're sure to succumb to the strange beauty of this rocky place. Let your imagination fly — and you may even sense the spirit of Geronimo lurking in the shadow.

From here you can retrace your steps, heading north on A-186 to Willcox and then going west on I-10 back to Tucson, or you can go on to see the ghost towns of Chochise County. If you plan to visit the ghost towns, you should plan to stay overnight in Benson or Willcox (SEE DAY TRIP 2, EAST FROM TUCSON).

DOS CABEZAS

This is one of several ghost towns in Cochise County. The others can be found in DAY TRIP 2, EAST FROM TUCSON. From Chiricahua National Monument, take A-186 north for nine miles to Dos Cabezas. During its mining heyday, this community was a stage station. Not quite a ghost town, Dos Cabezas supports enough people to maintain a U.S. post office. As you walk around, you'll get a sense of what this place felt like when gold fever raged through the region.

Day Trip 4

SAFFORD
WORTH MORE TIME:
ARAVAIPA CANYON

SAFFORD

From Tucson head east on I-10 to its junction with US-666. Go north on US 666 about 34 miles to Safford.

Dwarfed by the towering Mount Graham, which rises 10,713 feet above it, Safford has grown as an agricultural and copper mining community. Like many small Arizona towns, this Graham County community offers the casual visitor more outdoor than indoor activities.

Graham County was organized in 1881, but its history dates back to the Anasazi Indians, an ancient people who inhabited the area around the time of Christ. The Anasazi were followed by the Hohokams, farmers who disappeared in the 13th century, and finally by the Apaches who were nomadic fierce fighters. Although Coronado visited this area in 1540, it wasn't until tiny Camp Goodwin was established in 1864 that white men made their presence known in this area. Not surprisingly, the Apaches were not about to give up this land so easily and they battled to keep their territory. The last of the Apache chieftains, Geronimo, finally surrendered in 1888.

As you drive through the sculpted countryside with its broad valleys and secluded canyons, you will be enthralled by the strange, twisted beauty and may understand why the Apaches believed this landscape was worth fighting for.

WHERE TO GO

Mount Graham. About nine miles south of Safford, off US-666, you will see A-366, or Swift Trail. Turn right and follow this road for a spectacular journey to the summit of Mount Graham. Like the drive to Mount Lemmon, this one takes you through five of the seven ecological zones of western North America. You'll begin in desert cactus and end in mountainous aspen.

When you see a sharp right-hand turn leading to Marijilda Canyon, *don't* take it. This road is not recommended for passenger cars. (As you travel around Arizona, always obey a sign that says: "Not Recommended for Passenger Car (or Sedan) Travel." These roads can get rough to impassable *fast!*) Instead, continue on Swift Trail. The first 22 miles are paved but then the road becomes well-maintained gravel. With its many switchbacks, you'll need about two hours to make it to the top. As you traverse the 36 miles to the summit, you'll pass campgrounds — complete with showers — and picnic grounds. Pull off at the scenic turnouts to drink in the views.

Although the drive is worth the trip, Mount Graham has nine major trails to hike, once you ascend. Dutch Henry Trail originates at Ladybug Saddle; Ash Creek Trail begins at the summer-home area of Columbine at 9500 feet. You can pick up Grant Goudy Ridge Trail at Soldier Creek Campground. Try the Round-the-Mountain Trail, covering 14 miles and touching on some of the most popular features of the area, or High Peak Trail, originating a short distance southeast of Columbine at 9600 feet. In addition, you can hike Clark Peak Trail in the Taylor Pass and West Peak area, Bear Canyon Trail, Snake Trail and Arcadia Trail. Pick up information and trail guides at the Safford-Graham County Chamber of Commerce, 1111 Thatcher Blvd., Safford, AZ 85546. (602) 428-2511.

Kachina Mineral Springs Spa. Six miles south of Safford, just off US-666. For a relaxing interlude, soak up the natural hot mineral springs which come out of the ground at a hot 108° F. Bathe in tiled, Roman-style tubs. Enthusiasts believe that the stimulating combination of bathing, sweating and massage cleanses both the body and the mind. Fee. (602) 428-7212.

WORTH MORE TIME:
ARAVAIPA CANYON

You *must* contact the Bureau of Land Management (BLM) before making a trek into this jewel of a wilderness area, and there is a fee. Write to the Bureau of Land Management, 425 E. Fourth St., Safford, AZ 85546 or call (602) 428-4040.

To get to Aravaipa Canyon from Safford, take US-666 south to A-266. Follow A-266 west to Bonita and then pick up the secondary road to the village of Klondyke. Follow this road to the canyon entrance. Park your vehicle and proceed on foot.

This canyon is *not* for the casual hiker. Aravaipa is designated as a wilderness area; it is not a picnic ground. The area covers 4044 acres and offers hikers and backpackers a relaxing-to-challenging experience. Bring water and a trail map (which you receive when you contact the BLM), even if you plan to spend only a few hours in this desert splendor.

Today Aravaipa is such a tranquil place that it's difficult to remember its violent history. However, the confluence of Aravaipa Creek and the San Pedro River was the original site of Camp Grant (now Fort Grant). Although the U.S. Army swore that the Aravaipa Indians had not been responsible for raiding the white settlements, both the white men and the Papago Indians were unconvinced. In 1872, a group of Tucson citizens and Papagos approached the Aravaipa Reservation and, before the sun rose, massacred 85 men, women and children.

As you hike in the canyon, you'll be flanked by cliffs rising 700 feet or more on either side of you. In some areas you must squeeze through narrow stone hallways. If you choose to follow Aravaipa Creek, plan on having wet shoes at times. You'll be wise to move quietly and carry a good camera to catch much of the endangered wildlife. Bighorn sheep take refuge here, and the largest number of native fish in any stream in the state populate the water. Aravaipa is also a birdwatcher's paradise.

While hikers wax eloquent about an autumn backpacking trip into Aravaipa Canyon, enthusiasts insist it's ideal anytime of year.

To return to Tucson after such a full day, follow US-666 south to I-10 and head west back to the "Old Pueblo." Or you can go on to Chiricahua National Monument (DAY TRIP 3, EAST FROM TUCSON).

Day Trip 1

TOMBSTONE
BISBEE
SIERRA VISTA
CORONADO NATIONAL MEMORIAL
FORT HUACHUCA

Although this day trip can be done in one day, you may prefer this as a more leisurely two-day excursion. Plan to arrive in Tombstone by mid-morning and reach Bisbee by suppertime. Stay overnight in Bisbee and then drive on to Sierra Vista, Fort Huachuca and back to Tucson the following day.

Should you decide to cover this portion of southern Arizona in one day, know at the outset that you can't see everything described below. Choose carefully among the attractions. There is so much to see that if you aren't careful, you'll arrive home in the wee hours of the morning, overtired and oversatiated.

TOMBSTONE

Begin in familiar territory by taking I-10 east to Benson. At US-80, head south to Tombstone. Here's where all your Western fantasies will come true. This is "The Town Too Tough To Die." It's where Ed Schieffelin went prospecting in 1878 for silver, warned that all he would find in this Apache-infested land was his tombstone. Instead, he found one of the richest silver strikes in the country.

Tombstone is no false-front, made-up Western town. This is the *real* thing. Once it boasted a population of about 10,000 wild and respectable souls. Today the community caters to tourists, but all the legends are alive and well here. As you walk the dusty streets, you'll see the O.K. Corral, the Birdcage Theatre, the Crystal Palace and other historic sites. Tombstone *is* the Wild West preserved at its most raunchy and best. It personifies the frontier experience in those wild days before the century turned.

What was it like to live here? George Parsons, an early settler, noted in his diary in 1880 that, "A man will go to the devil pretty fast in Tombstone. Faro, whiskey and bad women will beat anyone." And Wyatt Earp once commented, "We had no YMCA's."

As you come into town on US-80, you'll hit Fremont Street. Park anywhere. Since the entire town is a living museum, you'll want to see this national historic site on foot.

Begin with a liberal dose of history. Stop at the **Tombstone Epitaph,** 5 South Fifth Ave., and pick up a map describing the points of interest.

Take a moment to familiarize yourself with the town. Most of what you'll want to tour lies within a few main streets. The sites are concentrated in a square framed by Fremont and Toughnut streets to the north and south, and Third and Fifth avenues on the west and east.

Since most of the attractions have an entrance fee, you may prefer to stop in at the O.K. Corral or Tombstone Historama and buy a combination ticket rather than pay separately for each. The combination ticket saves you a little money and a lot more time waiting to buy other tickets.

For more information before you go, write the Tombstone Tourism Association, 5 South Fifth Ave., Tombstone, AZ 85638, for a map and a brochure.

WHERE TO GO

Tombstone Courthouse. Toughnut Street between Third and Fourth avenues. This elegant structure was built in 1882 for the then amazing sum of $43,000. It served as the Cochise County Courthouse until 1929 when the county seat was moved to Bisbee. Two floors of exhibits await visitors. There's a ghoulish side-trip out the side door to see the hangman's platform, a room devoted to cattlemen, another to lawyers, and rooms full of costumes, jewelry and china. This is a good first stop to get you in the mood of the 1880s. Open daily. Fee. (602) 457-3311.

Tombstone Historama. Allen Street between Third and Fourth streets, next to the O.K. Corral. Enter this bright, airy building and slide back into time thanks to this unique, informative electronic presentation of Tombstone's history. You'll be seated in a small theater to watch an excellent mini sound and light production. You'll come away with a much better understanding of the forces which shaped this tough little town. Open daily. Fee. (602) 457-3456.

O.K. Corral. Allen Street between Third and Fourth avenues. This is where it all happened, where history was made that bloody, dusty October day in 1881 when the Earp brothers and Doc Holliday faced off against the Clanton and McLaury brothers. You'll see the lifelike figures in a major gunfight was staged in such a small space. Even non-Western history buffs will be strongly affected by this site. Open daily. Fee. (602) 457-3456.

Bird Cage Theatre. On Allen Street just east of Fifth Ave. Here tired miners bragged of strikes yet to come. Gamblers and gunmen cavorted. The law kept order and pretty young girls charmed them all. Preserved as it was in the 1880s, this theater was the gathering place for Tombstone citizens looking for fun. There's less glamour than you might expect, but remember that in the 1880s, this place was "it." Fee. Open daily. (602) 457-3421.

Rose Tree Inn Museum, Toughnut St. between Fourth and Fifth avenues. You'll see the world's largest rose bush, spread over 7000 square feet, which grew from one slip sent to a Scottish bride living in Tombstone. Inside the museum antique furnishings give visitors a glimpse of how people lived in Tombstone a century ago. Open daily. Fee. (602) 457-3326.

Crystal Palace Saloon. Allen St. and Fifth Ave. While the Birdcage Theatre was bawdy, the Crystal Palace was more refined. Here the elite and not-so-elite gathered for food and drink. Today you can belly up to the bar and eat and drink (both soft drinks and alcoholic) in the carefully preserved interior. Come for good food, atmosphere, and loud, vintage 1890s saloon music. Open daily. Fee. (602) 457-3611.

Tombstone Epitaph. Fifth Ave. near Fremont St. Visit the original newspaper building which continues to publish the famous *Tombstone Epitaph.* You can purchase a subscription for $7.00 to keep you up on Tombstone once you are home.

Boot Hill. You pass the sign to Boot Hill as you come into town on US-80. You can stop either on the way in or on your way out of town. Many infamous gunslingers are buried at Boot Hill. Read the epitaphs. They are wonderfully cryptic and humorous. Open daily. Donation suggested.

Tombstone has many other museums and points of interest. Depending upon your time and enthusiasm, spend a full day or just a few hours to get the flavor of this bawdy, rugged place.

WHERE TO EAT

Longhorn Restaurant. 501 Allen St. Come for breakfast, lunch or dinner and feast on Italian, Mexican and American food. Ask about the lunch special; it's always good. $$; □. (602) 457-3405.

Lucky Cuss. 414 Allen St. Sample food cooked the original, 1880s way on wood-burning stoves in this historically charming saloon. Slow-cooked ribs are their specialty. $$; □. (602) 457-3561.

WHERE TO STAY

Best Western Lookout Lodge. On US-80 about one mile northwest of town. This is the largest motel in the area, featuring 40 units and a swimming pool. Although there is no restaurant, a continental breakfast is served. US-80 W., P. O. Box 787, Tombstone, AZ 85638. $$; . (602) 457-2223.

BISBEE

Continue south about 25 miles on US-80 to Bisbee. Just six miles north of the Mexican border, this charming community is famous for its mountainous setting, steep, winding streets, and crazy patchwork of architectural building styles. You'll enter town on US-80 through Mule Pass Tunnel. A third of a mile long, it is Arizona's longest tunnel. As you get near town, watch for the Bisbee business loop which will be on your right. Follow it to Old Bisbee and you'll wind up on Main Street.

Bisbee has been described by Arizona writer, Joseph Stocker, as a "larger and newer version of Jerome." (SEE DAY TRIP 2, NORTH FROM PHOENIX). Like Jerome, Bisbee began as a mining town. During its heyday, this was *the* place to stop between New Orleans and San Francisco. Millions of tons of copper, gold and silver were pulled from the Mule Mountains surrounding the town. By the late 1880s, Bisbee offered every cultural, culinary and sporting diversion found in any major American city.

The Phelps Dodge Corporation closed its copper operations in Bisbee in the mid-1970s, but instead of dying, the community determined to survive as a tourism center in southeastern Arizona. During the late 1960s and the 1970s, hippies heard about the community and flocked here in droves, attracted by the temperate climate and inexpensive housing. Today most of the hippie culture has vanished, but some artists, poets and artisans remain in residence. Thanks to a strong dose of community spirit, Bisbee is succeeding as a tourist center, and visitors appreciate the blend of historical charm and modern-day convenience the town offers.

You'll want to wander around "Old Bisbee," as it's called. Don't be deceived by the sleepy facade. This isn't a living museum like Tombstone. Here you'll find a very much alive community populated with Bisbee-boosters. You'll enjoy touring the old residential sections where turn-of-the-century homes are squeezed onto narrow steep streets wedged into equally narrow, scenic canyons. The result is an intriguing web of tangled mountain roads and architecturally interesting structures.

If you can, take a complete walking tour of downtown. Stop in at the Chamber of Commerce, 78 Main St., and pick up a brochure. Even if your time is limited, plan to walk some of Bisbee's historical district to savor its history. If you aren't up to a strenuous stroll, take a bus tour of Old Bisbee and the hilly residential neighborhood known as the Warren area. Each tour lasts approximately one and one-half hours and allows you plenty of time to take pictures. Fee. For information regarding hours of departure, call (602) 432-2071.

WHERE TO GO

Queen Mine Tours. Number 1, Dart Road. To get to the Queen Mine building, drive or walk immediately south of Old Bisbee's business district off the US 80 interchange. Underground mine tours leave daily at scheduled hours. As you explore the mine with your guide, you'll hear about George Warren who, having celebrated with a few too many on the Fourth of July, bragged that he could outrun a horse and rider. In a burst of inebriated pluck, he bet his mining claim, the Copper Queen Mine, on the race. He ran and lost. Eventually his claim panned out, ultimately worth more than $40 million. Today George Warren's biggest claim to fame is that he was the model for the man who stands with his shovel in the center of the Arizona State Seal.

During this educational tour, you'll learn how Bisbee miners coaxed minerals from the mountains. Much of the original mining equipment stands in place. Although you walk into the Copper Queen, you'll ride out on small train cars. Bring a sweater. The mine remains a chilly 47° F. Open daily. Fee. For information about the time of tours, call (602) 432-2071.

Lavender Open Pit. Drive to a viewpoint on US-80 three-quarters of a mile beyond the Queen Mine building to see the open pit, or take a guided tour which leaves from the Queen Mine building every day at noon. As you gaze into this huge bowl scooped out of the landscape, you'll marvel at how man ever carved such an immense niche in the earth. Although the Lavender Open Pit shimmers with color, the name comes from a mine manager, Harry Lavender. Open daily. Fee. (602) 432-2071.

Brewery Gulch. 13-17 Brewery Ave. Also known as the Muheim Block, this street shoots dramatically uphill or downhill (depending upon your vantage point) from Howell Avenue. Completed in 1905, Brewery was once home to the Bisbee Stock Exchange, brothels, restaurants, lodging facilities and saloons. Now under restoration, it emits old echoes of wilder days when gamblers and miners traipsed up Brewery for excitement. Today visitors can poke through new shops and art galleries along this narrow street.

Old Phelps Dodge General Office Building. 5 Copper Queen Plaza. This structure was completed in 1895 and was designed as the general offices of the copper company. On the National Register of Historic Landmarks, the Old Phelps Dodge building is located in Bisbee's "Grassy Park." It is now the town's Mining and Historical Museum. Here you can see early mining equipment and a diorama describing a mining operation. In another setting, such a display may not excite you, but it springs to life in Bisbee. Free. (602) 432-7071.

Covenant Presbyterian Church. 19 Howell Ave. Next to the Copper Queen Hotel, this imposing European-style church was built in 1903. At the time it was built, a 579-pipe organ was installed. Over the years the organ has been enlarged and it remains in excellent condition. Free. (602) 432-4327.

WHERE TO EAT AND STAY

Copper Queen Hotel. 713 Howell Ave. Have breakfast, lunch or dinner at the Copper Queen. Dine outdoors at the patio cafe or sit inside in the historic, restored dining room. The varied menu features old-fashioned American food spiced with a liberal dash of Mexican.

The rooms are large and each one is different. Some bathtubs still have feet attached. In short, there is a distinct flavor of a bygone era at this restored hotel. While the Copper Queen may not be as luxuriously quaint as you might wish, it is authentic. What's more, it offers a change from contemporary hotel/motel sameness. When you sleep here, know you are in good company. Theodore Roosevelt stayed at the Copper Queen; so did General John J. Pershing when he was on his way to Mexico to catch up with Pancho Villa. The Copper Queen, P. O. Box CQ, Bisbee, AZ 85603. $$; □. (602) 432-2216.

SIERRA VISTA

From Bisbee, backtrack nine miles north on US-80 and follow A-90 west 20 miles to Sierra Vista. Perched at an elevation of 4623 feet, this fast-growing city is nestled on the slopes of the Huachuca Mountains. Surrounded on all sides by mountain ranges and never-ending views of the San Pedro Valley, the climate is as awesome as the scenery. Sierra Vista ranks as one of the three most temperate regions in the nation and its cool summers and moderate winters make this city increasingly popular with newcomers and tourists.

With an abundance of outdoor pleasures nearby, (everything from hiking trails to ghost towns and a mountain lake), Sierra Vista has become an important southern Arizona town. In the past, its biggest claim to fame was nearby Fort Huachuca. While the economy remains closely tied to the military installation, Sierra Vista is establishing itself as a manufacturing, wholesale and retail center.

WHERE TO GO

The Mile Hi/Ramsey Canyon Preserve. Six miles south of Sierra Vista on A-92. Turn right onto Ramsey Canyon Road and drive four miles to The Mile Hi. This small and limited facility, owned by the Nature Conservancy, is sheltered in a deep gorge within 280 acres of the Huachuca Mountains. It's a favorite place for birdwatchers and others who are interested in learning more about this unique, fragile environment. Should you decide to spend time here, try to arrive on a weekday. It's much less crowded then, and you'll have more opportunity to walk the two nature trails and enjoy the serenity of this preserve.

Both nature trails open windows to a world populated by a great variety of birds, reptiles and animals. Guided hikes can be arranged by contacting the Ramsey Canyon Preserve manager in advance. There's also a bookstore, gift shop and nature reference library on the grounds.

When you plan a trip here, remember that not every type of bird can be seen at the canyon during all times of the year. Ramsey Canyon is known as a hummingbird sanctuary, but these delicate creatures are here only from April through August. During the winter, they migrate further south.

Because of the comparatively small size and ecological fragility of the area, certain rules are strictly enforced. No picnicking is allowed within the confines of the preserve and parking is extremely limited. RV's and campers cannot be accommodated. Whenever possible, car pooling is encouraged. In addition, pets are not allowed on the property. Visitor hours are strictly enforced. For more information, contact The Mile Hi, R.R. 1, Box 84, Hereford, AZ 85615. The preserve is open daily from 8 a.m. to 5 p.m. Free. (602) 378-2785.

WHERE TO STAY

The Mile Hi. Ramsey Canyon Preserve. This is the only Nature Conservancy in the country with overnight accommodations on the grounds. The name, The Mile Hi, comes from a private ranch the conservancy bought in 1975. As a result of this purchase, six cabins are available for rental. Each comes equipped with outdoor barbecue grill, picnic table, fully equipped kitchens and linens. You'll need to bring your own food. Although you may rent the cabins by the day or week, during the spring and summer months you must reserve cabins for a minimum of three nights. Call in advance, or write to The Mile Hi, R.R. 1, Box 84, Hereford, AZ 85615. No cards. (602) 378-2785.

CORONADO NATIONAL MEMORIAL

Located 20 miles south of Sierra Vista off A-92, Coronado National Memorial salutes the Spanish explorer Francisco Vasquez de Coronado, who searched for the Seven Cities of Cibola looking for gold.

From Sierra Vista head south on A-92. Turn west onto Montezuma Canyon Road and continue for five miles until you come to the visitors center and museum. The road is paved for just about a mile west of the visitors center, and then it becomes a mountainous gravel path which leads to Montezuma Pass, a narrow passage way over the Huachuca Mountains. Park here and pick up the hiking trail of your choice. From the pass, you can gaze west over the San Rafael Valley and Patagonia Mountains toward Nogales (see DAY TRIP 1, SOUTH OF TUCSON).

The Coronado National Memorial is the name given to this entire area and includes both natural and man-made historical features. There is no plaque or statue commemorating Coronado's adventures. Instead, hiking trails lace the 4976 acres which are home to a variety of birds, animals and plants.

Told that cities existed where streets were paved with gold, Coronado arrived in Mexico in 1535. On February 23, 1540, he headed north with 336 Spanish soldiers and four priests to search for treasure. Instead of finding golden cities, Coronado found mud houses — adobe pueblos — inhabited by Indians. Pushing on, he ultimately came upon Hopi Indian villages in northeastern Arizona. Driven by the promise of gold, he continued to search past Acoma and onwards to the upper Pecos River. Finally, discredited and disheartened, Coronado admitted defeat and died in relative obscurity. Although he never found gold, Coronado did change the course of Southwestern history. The Spaniard left behind horses which helped the Indians dominate the plains and mountains, and he introduced the white man's religion to this region. Historians agree that the Coronado expedition formed the basis for contemporary Hispanic-American culture. Open daily. Free. (602) 458-9333.

FORT HUACHUCA

From the Coronado National Memorial return to Sierra Vista on A-92, then drive west for four miles to Fort Huachuca. To get to the main gate follow A-90 south to where it intersects with Squier Avenue. The main gate is on the corner of Squier Avenue and A-90.

This 73,000-acre installation lies within the boundaries of Cochise and Santa Cruz counties and is closely tied to the history of Arizona. Now the largest employer in southern Arizona, Fort Huachuca was established in 1877 as a base for American soldiers during the Indian wars of the 1870s and 1880s. Fresh running water, high ground and shade trees convinced the Army that this was a wise location for a fort. When Geronimo surrendered and the Indian hostilities ended, Fort Huachuca was kept active to guard against problems around the Mexican border.

Many well-known units were stationed here, but the most famous is the "Buffalo Soldiers," the 10th Cavalry Division of Black fighters who accompanied General Pershing when he chased Pancho Villa into Mexico in 1916.

Closed down after World War II, Fort Huachuca was later reactivated and in 1953 became the home of the U.S. Army Electronic Proving Ground. Again, its physical setting saved the fort because the mild, dry climate and open spaces made it a natural for the electronics field. Today the base buzzes as a center for intelligence and worldwide communications. Open daily. For information regarding the base, write: Headquarters, Fort Huachuca, ATTN: CCH-PTS-PM, Fort Huachuca, AZ 85613. (602) 538-3638.

WHERE TO GO

Fort Huachuca Historical Museum. Corner of Boyd and Grierson streets, overlooking the Brown Parade Field. The museum is housed on the historic Old Post where almost all of the original buildings are still in use. Opened in 1960, the museum tells the story of Fort Huachuca and of southwestern Arizona. It showcases military memorabilia from the 1800s to the present. Because Arizona history is closely tied to the military, the exhibits will help you understand events leading up to this young territory becoming the 48th state. There's ample parking, and a gift shop features items and books related to the Southwest. Open daily. Free. (602) 538-5736.

To return to Tucson from Fort Huachuca, drive north on A-90 to I-10, then west on I-10 to Tucson.

Day Trip 1

SONOITA
PATAGONIA
NOGALES, ARIZONA, UNITED STATES
AND NOGALES, SONORA, MEXICO
TUMACACORI
TUBAC

If you decide to stay overnight in Tombstone (see DAY TRIP 1, SOUTHEAST OF TUCSON) you can start this day trip by heading south the next morning. Follow US-80 north of Tombstone to A-82 and continue west on A-82 to Sonoita and then south on A-82 to Patagonia and Nogales. You can return to Tucson by driving north on I-19, stopping at Tumacacori and Tubac on your way back. This makes a pleasantly packed two- or three-day mini-vacation. Spend the first night in Bisbee, the second in Tombstone, and arrive in Tucson the third evening.

If you make this trip in a single day from Tucson, plan on a long, full day to travel to the Mexican border and return to the Old Pueblo. Everybody likes to visit Mexico at least once while in Arizona. What makes this trip easier than most Mexican vacations is that you don't drive across the border. You'll park in Nogales, Arizona, and walk across the international line into Nogales, Mexico. Once you leave Arizona and enter the state of Sonora, Mexico, you'll feel worlds away from the United States. Border towns are usually safe as long as you stay on the main streets. If you're a naturalized citizen or not an American citizen, be sure to bring your *proof of citizenship* or *passport* so that you can re-enter the United States!

SONOITA

From Tucson take the scenic drive to Nogales by heading southeast on I-10, then south on A-83 for 27 miles to Sonoita. This route takes you through magnificent country, studded with cactus, beveled with foothills, and ringed with wide, open valleys. Even during the summer, when the rest of the Arizona desert is bleached to a coarse yellow, the high grasses of this area retain their green tint.

Sonoita is an old community which dates to around 1699. Originally it was the site of a Visita, a mission that only occasionally received personal visits by Spanish padres. Today this small community welcomes visitors who are taking what locals call the "back" way — the more scenic, non interstate trip — to Nogales. Continue south past Sonoita to Patagonia.

PATAGONIA

Another tiny Arizona town, Patagonia lies in a narrow valley bounded by the Santa Rita Mountains to the north and the Patagonias to the south. The mountains and the town were named after the now-closed Patagonia Silver Mine which operated there in 1858. Also known as the Mowry Mine after Sylvester Mowry purchased it in the 1850s, it produced more than $1.5 million worth of ore during its heyday. By the early 1900s the veins were too diminished to merit any more activity.

Today Patagonia has some of the finest quarter horse and cattle ranches in the Southwest. It is known throughout the state for its inviting location and, thanks to its higher elevation, slightly cooler temperatures. Most people pass through Patagonia, hurrying to get to Nogales, but there is one attraction worth stopping to see and a good place to eat in town. Since there are only two major streets, McKeown Avenue and A-82, you can't get lost in "downtown" Patagonia.

WHERE TO GO

The Museum of the Horse. McKeown Avenue off A-82. Anne Stradling's collection of horse memorabilia was opened to the public in 1960. Since then, this unique museum has continued to grow in popularity and size. You'll find more than 45 horse-drawn vehicles and saddles, harnesses, bits and spurs from around the world as well as fine paintings by such famous artists as Frederic Remington, C. M. Russell and Frank Tenney Johnson. This small but appealing place should fascinate anyone who loves horses. Open daily. Fee. (602) 394-2264.

The Patagonia-Sonoita Creek Sanctuary. South of Patagonia on A-82 between Patagonia and Nogales. As you enter Patagonia on A-82, watch for the Stage Stop Inn and the Patagonia Market. Turn right onto Third Avenue. You may want to stop at the filling station in town to use the restrooms since there are no facilities at the sanctuary. Continue south on Third Avenue to Pennsylvania Avenue and turn east onto Pennsylvania. Follow the road across a small creek and watch for signs which say "Nature Conservancy." (The conservancy operates the sanctuary.) Look for Gate 2, which will be on your left. Turn in and drive to the **Information Center.** All visitors must register at an entrance gate.

Birdwatchers and naturalists flock to this 312-acre preserve. Located in a narrow flood plain, the sanctuary features a majestic stand of cottonwood trees interspersed with Arizona walnut and velvet ash. Avid bird-watchers from all over the world know that this is the place to see more than 200 species.

To protect the fragile character of the sanctuary, rules are strictly enforced. Pets are not allowed on the grounds. There is no picnicking, no camping or fires, and no motorized vehicles allowed on trails within the conservancy. Opened daily. Free. For more information, contact the Nature Conservancy, 30 North Tucson Boulevard, Tucson, AZ 85716, or call (602) 327-4478.

WHERE TO EAT

Stage Stop Inn. McKeown Avenue off A-82 (next to the Museum of the Horse). People come from far and wide to eat at the Stage Stop Inn. The complete menu and home-baked goods keep long-term guests and casual visitors happy. If you're in town on Sunday, indulge yourself at the Sunday buffet, well-known throughout the area for its variety and abundance. The seafood salad is a special favorite.

You can come for one night or stay as long as four months in one of 43 spacious, airy guest rooms. For information, write the Stage Stop Inn, Box 777, Patagonia, AZ 85624. $$; □. (602) 394-2211.

NOGALES, ARIZONA, U.S. AND NOGALES, SONORA, MEXICO

South on A-82 are the twin cities of Nogales, Arizona and Nogales, Sonora, Mexico. As you round the bend in the road, you'll see both cities nestled in a narrow valley. Notice the colors of the houses on the Mexican side and how different the two cities look even from a distance. As you continue into town, you'll be in the heart of Nogales, Arizona, where A-89 and A-82 join I-19.

The community on this side is a bustling place complete with a good manufacturing and retail base. Nogales, Sonora, is an equally active area. The Mexican city projects a south-of-the-border feeling. Even though you're only a few feet into Mexico, the mañana atmosphere prevails here, and the more you compare the two cities, the more you'll realize how far away Arizona seems once you step across the international line. This is Old Mexico with bull fights, fiestas and streets lined with small shops.

The border is always teeming with cars and trucks which are jammed with people and packages. Some of the guards will check every package thoroughly, so allow enough time to get across the border on the return trip.

It's recommended that you park your car on the Arizona side and do not attempt to drive into Mexico. Obey signs and don't park illegally. Parking is usually available by the railroad tracks on the Arizona side and you can proceed across the border on foot. Should you decide to drive into Mexico, take out Mexican automobile insurance first, since United States insurance doesn't cover you in foreign countries. You can buy Mexican car insurance by the day in Tucson or in Nogales, Arizona, at several agencies.

WHERE TO GO

In Mexico walk up any of the main streets in Nogales and browse. You'll find good shops on Elias Calles, Lopez Mateos and Obregon avenues and on Hidalgo Street. Think of the shopping area as a long rectangle bounded by Elias Calles Avenue and Hidalgo Street, stretching from the border to Andonegui Street. Look for good buys on pottery, baskets, leather, wrought iron and Mexican silver. You can also find lovely embroidered clothing as well as linens and crystal. Remember, this is Mexico and you are expected to bargain! Take your time and look around. You'll find the shop owners friendly and happy to make your trip worthwhile.

When you buy in Nogales, you'll deal in U.S. dollars. When you return to the United States you must verbally declare your U.S. citizenship and purchases. You are allowed to bring back up to $400 of merchandise duty free, including one quart of liquor and one carton of cigarettes per adult.

La Roca. 91 Elias St., Nogales, Sonora. After you cross the border, turn left and cross over the railroad tracks. Continue two blocks, turn right onto Elias Street, and walk two more blocks to La Roca, an elegant, enclosed shopping center resembling a large pinkish-red, adobe-style hotel. Inside you'll find more expensive items than on the main shopping streets. Most shopkeepers here accept credit cards. You'll encounter some rough sidewalks and high curbs en route to La Roca, so be careful where you walk.

WHERE TO EAT

La Roca. 91 Elias Street. Mexican food is an obvious specialty here. The upstairs dining room offers margaritas and nachos as well as complete lunches and dinners. $-$$. □. 2-0760 (Mexico.)

TUMACACORI NATIONAL MONUMENT

After touring Mexico, head north on I-19 to Tucson, or stop at Tumacacori and Tubac.

The Tumacacori mission is a national monument which rises from the desert floor like a half-finished symphony. Built by the Franciscans around 1800, for five years this church was a functioning religious center. Then the Franciscans were expelled and the church was abandoned. Unattended, the mission was gutted repeatedly by Apaches and fortune hunters.

In 1929 the National Park Service restored it to its former, if unfinished, glory. Visitors can take a self-guided tour and see a scale model of how Tumacacori might have looked around 1820. If you call ahead, arrange a guided tour. For information, write Tumacacori National Monument, P.O. Box 67, Tumacacori, AZ 85640. Open every day except Christmas. Fee. (602) 398-2341.

TUBAC

Continue north three miles on I-19 and take Exit 34 to the village of Tubac. Forty-five miles south of Tucson, Tubac is touted as the place where "art and history meet." For once, hype is not far from the truth for Tubac is a unique artistic community.

While the old world of Tubac exerts a mystical pull, visitors also will be lured by the new. Thanks to Dale Nichols who opened an art school here in 1948, Tubac continues to attract artists and artisans. Potters, brush and palette painters, and designers of batik, gold, silver and wood carving have, over the years, "discovered" Tubac. As a result the town is a mecca for art lovers. More than 50 galleries and studios tempt travelers.

The first European settlement in Arizona, Tubac lays claim to having the first newspaper, the first Spanish land grant and Arizona's first state park. Even without all these "firsts," the history of the area is fascinating. It dates back some 10,000 years when the Hohokam Indians farmed here. They were followed by the Ootam (now called the Pimas and the Papagos) and eventually by the Spaniards who arrived with Father Kino in 1691. Tubac became part of Mexico in 1821 and with the Gadsden purchase, slipped into American hands in 1856.

WHERE TO GO

The Presidio Museum and Ruins. Tubac Presidio State Park. As you continue on Tubac Road past the business area, it becomes Wilson Road after it crosses Burruel Street. Then, as it curves toward the Presidio, it is called Presidio Drive.

The Presidio Museum offers a glimpse into life in a Spanish fort around 1750. An underground exhibit includes some of the original wall and floor. Open daily from October to May. It's best to call ahead to inquire about summer hours. Fee. (602) 389-2371.

WHERE TO EAT AND STAY

The Tubac Country Club. P.O. Box 1353, Tubac, AZ 85646. When you take the Tubac exit off I-19, continue north on Frontage Road for one and one-half miles. The public is welcome at the club restaurant, which offers the most relaxing place to eat between Tucson and Nogales. The menu is mostly American, although some south-of-the-border dishes are included.

This picturesque resort sports a golf course and hotel accommodations surrounded by patio homes. Book a room by the day, week or for the entire season. Reservations are suggested in the summer and necessary during the rest of the year. $$; ☐. (602) 398-2211.

WHERE TO SHOP

Gift shops, arts and crafts galleries, and boutiques are clustered within an area bounded by Tubac Road and Camino Otero, Calle Baca and Presidio Drive. Here you find many one-of-a-kind items created by local residents. Most shops are open Monday through Saturday, and many have Sunday hours as well. Ask for a free illustrated map of the area at any store.

Tubac Center of the Arts. Plaza Road (there are no street addresses in Tubac). As you head toward Tubac on Frontage Road, Plaza Road intersects with Frontage. You're welcome to browse during the season, October through May. This is the home of the Santa Cruz Valley Art Association which showcases a variety of styles and types of art by local painters, sculptors, and craftspersons. The center is open Tuesday through Saturday from October through May. Donations are suggested. (602) 398-2371.

Day Trip 1

KITT PEAK AND
KITT PEAK NATIONAL OBSERVATORY

KITT PEAK AND KITT PEAK NATIONAL OBSERVATORY

From Tucson pick up A-86 (Ajo Highway) and follow that southwest for 37 miles. At the junction of A-386, turn left (the only way you can) and begin the 12.2-mile climb to Kitt Peak. Although this is an excellent road, it twists and winds around the mountain, giving passengers sometimes breathtaking views of sheer drop-offs and broad valleys.

The Kitt Peak National Observatory is located on top of Kitt Peak in the Quinlan Mountains. At an elevation of 6882 feet, this giant eye-in-the-sky houses the largest concentration of facilities for stellar and solar research in the world. The primary mission of Kitt Peak National Observatory is optical astronomical research. Solar astronomers work from sunrise to sunset; stellar and planetary astronomers work during the hours of darkness but also, thanks to special scientific equipment, during daylight.

Scientists from all over the world regularly visit Kitt Peak. Although the astronomy center employs over 50 people, only the necessary support staff lives on the mountain top. The rest make the daily round-trip to the summit. There is plenty for the public to see here. You can spend an hour or a full day, depending upon your interest in astronomy.

Stop first at the visitors center. You can pick up an illustrated brochure for a self-guided walk, or you can join one of the regularly scheduled tours conducted twice daily, including weekends, which begin at the visitors center. You also will find exhibits and models to study, films to watch, and even a model of the large telescope which you can operate.

As you walk out of the visitors center, look out over Altar Valley. Some 18 miles to the southwest, you will see Sells, headquarters of the Papago tribe. Due south, there is a dome-shaped mountain peak called Baboquivari, the traditional home of the Papago Indian God I-I'toy.

While at the Kitt Peak National Observatory, you'll want to see the McMath Solar Telescope, which is the largest solar telescope in the world. It is always aligned with the celestial North Pole at Tucson's latitude, and the entire structure housing it is encased in copper. Coolants are piped through the scope's outer casing or "skin" as it is called, to insure that this sensitive instrument is maintained in a uniform temperature.

Another fascinating device to see is the Nicholas U. Mayall Four-Meter Telescope, the nation's second-largest optical instrument. It allows astronomers to study objects six million times fainter than the dimmest star visible with the naked eye.

Only candy and soft drinks are sold on Kitt Peak, so if you decide to make a day of it, pack a picnic lunch. Follow the signs to the picnic area, complete with tables and fire pits.

Since it's usually about 15 degrees cooler at the top of the mountain than in Tucson, take a jacket or sweater.

Kitt Peak Observatory is open daily. Free. For more information, including arrangements for group tours, write to National Optical Astronomy Observatories (Kitt Peak National Observatory), 950 North Cherry, Tucson, AZ 85726-6732, or call (602) 325-9200.

Day Trip 1

MISSION OF SAN XAVIER DEL BAC
OLD TUCSON
ARIZONA-SONORA MUSEUM
SAGUARO NATIONAL MONUMENT (WEST)

Just 14 miles from Tucson is a cluster of worthwhile attractions. This day trip takes you through one of the most majestic forests of saguaro cacti you'll ever see. You can spend a full day of glitz and glamour combined with a liberal dose of science and education and unparalleled natural beauty. Visit each of these attractions in separate half-day trips and spend a few hours, or even an entire day, seeing each of them. Or, if you decide to take in all four at once, be ready for a long, full day — not because the distances are great, but because there's so much to see at each destination.

MISSION OF SAN XAVIER DEL BAC

Pick up I-19 and head south for this nine-mile trip through Tucson and South Tucson to San Xavier del Bac (Ha-veer). At Valencia Road, turn west and enter the San Xavier Indian reservation. Small houses and broad, tilled fields stretch in all directions.

In the distance, you will see the White Dove (as it's called) rise dramatically from the desert floor. Dazzling white, San Xavier shimmers like a bird caught between the brown-beige land and indigo sky. With its imposing dome and lofty parapets and towers, the Mission contrasts brilliantly against the violet of the nearby mountains. You'll quickly see why it has been called the finest example of mission architecture in the United States.

Turn south at Mission Road and follow it to the church. Constructed over a period of 14 years, from 1783 to 1797, San Xavier is a graceful blend of Moorish, Byzantine and late Mexican Renaissance styles. Mass is celebrated daily every morning and in three services on Sunday. A vital, living mission, this Church is used regularly by the nearby Papago and San Xavier Indians. (The vast Papago reservation is just west of the San Xavier land.)

Stand outside and contemplate the structure. The entire building is a series of domes and arches, and every surface is intricately adorned. Notice that wood was used only in the door and window frames. Look carefully to see a cat and a mouse carved into the facade of the building, one in each tower. Legend has it that if the cat ever catches the mouse, the world will end.

Walk inside. As your eyes become accustomed to the interior of the church, you'll see that while the colors have faded over the years, remnants of a once-vivid decor remain. Statues and original paintings give it a warm lived-in feeling.

Father Kino, a Jesuit padre widely revered in this area, visited this site in 1692. The padre laid the foundations for the first church, which was two miles north of the present mission and named it San Xavier in honor of his chosen patron, St. Francis Xavier who was the illustrious Jesuit "Apostle of the Indies." The reclining statue to your left, as you face the main altar, is Saint Francis Xavier.

To many people in the Southwest, this image of St. Francis Xavier has become a place of pilgrimage. If possible, plan to sit a while inside the church and experience the special ambience.

Outside once again, visit the mortuary chapel and then climb the hill east of the mission to see the replica of the grotto in Lourdes, France. Be sure to pick up a brochure as you enter the church for a more detailed explanation of the history of San Xavier del Bac. Open daily. No fee, although donations are accepted. (602) 294-2624.

OLD TUCSON

Old Tucson. 201 S. Kinney Road. From San Xavier, travel north on Mission Road to Ajo Road (A-86). Take Ajo Road west to Kinney Road. Follow Kinney north to Old Tucson.

If you are coming from Tucson, rather than from San Xavier, drive west on Speedway Boulevard to where it joins Anklam Road and becomes Gates Pass Road. As you continue west, you'll climb quickly into the foothills of the Tucson Mountains. Soon you'll be engulfed by the desert. As you get near Gates Pass, the road will twist and dip and climb until even the sky seems filled with mountains and saguaros. Once you are over the mountain top, you'll gently descend into the valley. Watch for Kinney

Road to your left. You'll turn south on Kinney and follow that a few miles to Old Tucson. If you are driving a large motor home or towing a trailer, take the Ajo Road-Kinney Road route and avoid Gates Pass.

The second-most visited attraction in the state (the Grand Canyon is first), Old Tucson is great fun for the entire family. Youngsters and oldsters will get a kick out of the almost-real gunfights. There are movie sets to ogle and a narrow-gauge railroad that takes you around the grounds. Enjoy amusement park rides, climb aboard a stage coach, or take a tour behind a sound stage. Naturally, it's a little bit fake, but, after all, Old Tucson never pretended to be authentic.

Built originally in 1939 as a set for the epic movie, *Arizona*, this location continues to attract crowds. Cinematographers and tourists love the place. Since *Arizona*, more than 100 other movies, television shows and national commercials have used Old Tucson as a setting. Open daily. Fee. (602) 883-0100.

ARIZONA-SONORA DESERT MUSEUM

The museum is on Kinney Road. From Old Tucson head north on Kinney Road. Continue on Kinney as it bends northwest and follow the signs to the entrance of the Arizona-Sonora Desert Museum.

If you think of museums as stodgy places you visit when it rains, think again. This one has a well-defined mission: to tell the story of life in the Sonoran Desert and of all the creatures who call this region home. An exciting combination of a zoo, an aquarium and a botanical garden, this one-of-a-kind place defies a simple definition.

Look carefully. You'll see samples of nearly everything that crawls, runs, climbs, flies or slithers in the desert as well as a wondrous display of plants indigenous to this special environment. Some are gorgeous; others almost grotesque. If you've ever wondered what a Boojum tree looks like, this is the place to see one.

Stroll along manicured garden paths to see well-designed, educational exhibits.

With the addition of the Earth Sciences Center, the Desert Museum has created an exhibit which mimics the underworld. Through an ingenious display, it opens this little-seen place to visitors. There's even an imitation limestone cave where stalactites and stalagmites "grow."

Another section of the Earth Sciences Center transports you back billions of years to the time when the desert began. Thanks to films, photographs and maps, this exhibit enables you to understand how this part of the world was formed.

Before you leave the museum grounds, be sure to browse through the gift shop which is filled with various arts, crafts and scientific displays.

If you have time to see only one museum in southern Arizona, this is the place to visit. To make your day more enjoyable, try to arrive during the morning so you can observe the creatures when they are most active. (Like all smart residents of the desert, they siesta in the afternoon.) Please leave your pets at home. Temperatures in unventilated vehicles, especially during the summer, can be fatal to animals. Fee. Open daily from 8:30 a.m. to sundown. Call for special summer hours. (602) 883-1380. Route 9, Box 900, Tucson, AZ 85743-9989.

SAGUARO NATIONAL MONUMENT
(WEST)

This is the western (Tucson Mountain) park of Saguaro National Monument. (see DAY TRIP 1, EAST FROM TUCSON for information on the eastern Rincon unit.) There are two parks which make up Saguaro National Monument: one lies to the east of Tucson, and the other to the west. Both are worth your time.

As you leave the Arizona-Sonora Desert Museum, continue northwest on Kinney Road to the Red Hills Information Center in the Tucson Mountain section of the Saguaro National Monument. Pick up a map of the national monument at the information center, or sightsee from your car by taking the Bajado Loop drive. To do this, continue on Kinney Road until it becomes Golden Gate Road. Follow this road until you see Hohokam Road to your right. Take Hohokam Road south back to where it meets Kinney.

If you aren't walked out from Old Tucson and the Desert Museum, there are several good hiking trails, some of which lead to the 1429-foot-high **Wasson Peak.**

This section of Saguaro National Monument is slightly smaller than the Rincon Mountain area. However, the 21,078 acres contain an unusually dense and vigorous saguaro forest. The cacti, coupled with dramatic foothills and mountain views, make this a favorite photographic and relaxation stop. Although firewood and water are not available in the park, you will find picnic areas, scenic overlooks and restrooms. At the end of a long day you may be happy to just drive through and save the hiking for another time. Open daily. Free. (602) 883-6366.

From Saguaro National Monument, it's an easy trip south on Kinney to either Gates Pass Road or Ajo Road to Tucson.

Day Trip 1

PHOENIX

PHOENIX

From Tucson, follow I-10 northwest to Phoenix. This is an easy freeway drive which takes two or two and a half hours.

Contemporary Phoenix cherishes its desert, water supply, sunshine and famous leisure life-style. A fine climate translates into the good life. With 3,177,016 acres of city, state and county parks, federal lands and fresh water lakes within one hour's drive, play's the thing in Phoenix. Outdoor sports are de rigueur here. People jog, climb, swim and bike all year long. Everyone who stays comes to appreciate the natural setting. Men who didn't know a maple from an oak tree when they lived "back East," move to Phoenix and become connoisseurs of cactus.

In the old legend, the Phoenix bird spread her wings and rose from the ashes. Today's version stars its own legendary "bird" — the construction crane. The city is growing fast. Some look at the spread-out shape of Phoenix and call it "urban sprawl." Others smile and say that's what they moved west for — space.

Even with all the development, there's plenty of room here. The 13,000-acre South Mountain Park is the largest municipally-owned facility in the world. Squaw Peak, the Phoenix Mountain Preserve and North Mountain Parks each provide many more thousands of recreational acres.

Yet with all its emphasis on the big and the new, Phoenix is equally proud of its beginnings. A former mayor spearheaded the move to restore and dedicate a special section of downtown as Heritage Square. A stretch of freeway leading to Sky Harbor Airport, called the Hohokam, is painted with designs derived from ancient Indian symbols.

As you approach Phoenix, don't be put off by its size. It's an easy town to get around. Washington Street runs east and west and is the zero ("0"), or starting, point for all north and south addresses. Central Avenue runs north and south and is the starting point ("0") for east and west addresses. East of Central, the roads are labeled as streets, while west of Central they are called avenues. Keep this in mind and you won't find yourself at 35th Avenue looking for a number which is on 35th Street.

Stop first at the Phoenix & Valley of the Sun Convention & Visitors Bureau, 4455 East Camelback Rd., Suite 146, or call (602) 952-8687. Here you can inquire about accommodations, attractions, special events and dining and pick up brochures describing these in more detail.

WHERE TO GO

Following is a sample of what Phoenix has in store for visitors. For a more complete listing, read the brochures from the Phoenix & Valley of the Sun Convention & Visitors Bureau.

The Old State Capitol. 1700 W. Washington St. Pick up Washington in downtown Phoenix and follow it directly west to the Capitol Building. There is ample free parking in two large lots on the east side of 17th Avenue. When you park and turn toward the west, you'll be facing the Old Capitol building. You'll know it by the copper dome. Inside is a museum which features an exhibit of territorial and Arizona history and government. You can take either a self-guided or guided tour. This is a recommended trip for people who have a strong interest in the state. Open weekdays. Free. Call for tour hours. (602) 255-4900 and ask to be connected to the Museum.

Heritage Square. Sixth Street and Monroe St. In this area, you'll find the best of the old, and, with hotels and the convention center looming nearby, the most dazzling of the new that symbolize contemporary Phoenix. The centerpiece of Heritage Square is the **Rosson House,** a restored home built in 1894. With its spires and turrets, it casts a benevolent shadow on downtown. Surrounded by other houses, including the **Silva House, Stevens House** and **Stevens-Haugsten House,** and topped off with the airy **Lath House,** Heritage Square has become a favorite gathering place for residents and tourists.

As you walk through this charming block of homes you'll be transported to a gracious time when people slept on open sleeping porches to survive the desert summer, and ladies fanned themselves and sipped cool lemonade. A fee is charged to tour the Rosson House, but the others are open daily free of charge. (602) 262-5071.

The Civic Plaza. 225 E. Adams St., Phoenix. From the Rosson House, you can walk west to the Civic Plaza which contains the **Phoenix Civic Plaza Convention Center and Symphony Hall.** Both are focal points for business and entertainment for the entire valley. The convention center can host the world's largest conventions and top-name talent is booked into Symphony Hall throughout the year. Don't miss the elegant life-sized sculptures of dancers on the plaza. These are the work of Arizona artist John Waddell, a nationally-acclaimed sculptor. Parking is available under the Civic Plaza complex. For more information on the convention center, call (602) 252-6823. To inquire about events at Symphony Hall, call (602) 262-7272.

The Phoenix Art Museum. 1625 N. Central Ave., on the corner of Central Avenue and McDowell Rd. Long known for its fine collections of both Oriental and Mexican art, the museum also is home to an impressive collection of Western American art. Each October the Cowboy Artists of America ride into Phoenix to hold their annual show and sale at this facility. The museum's permanent collection concentrates on 18th and 19th century American and European art and sculpture. There is a distinguished collection of exquisitely detailed Thorne Miniature Rooms and the museum is home to the Arizona Costume Institute, which affords this facility an elegant display of period clothing.

Over the years, this museum has grown dramatically. In addition to the museum's own collection, visitors can view fine traveling exhibitions scheduled throughout the year. Tours led by museum docents are available by special arrangement. The museum shop is a good place to find unusual gift items and art books. Open daily except Monday. Fee. (602) 257-1222.

The Heard Museum. 22 E. Monte Vista Rd. There's free trolley service between the Phoenix Art Museum, the Heard Museum and the Spaghetti Company restaurant. The restaurant is located on Central Avenue and is a fun place to eat. Call the Heard to check on hours. Considered one of the finest anthropological museums in the world, the Heard has an impressive permanent collection, an inspiring audiovisual exhibit and important traveling shows. All of this excitement is encased in a lovely Hacienda-style building which shows off old Phoenix at its best.

Your first stop should be the audiovisual production shown in the main gallery. Sit on a bench and lose yourself in this 30-minute experience, "Our Voices, Our Land." As you watch and listen, you'll begin to understand something of the deep relationship which exists between the Indian people and their lands.

After the show, continue through the gallery. There's a time-line on the wall which graphically traces the development of the Southwest from the Paleo-Indian era (c. 1500 B.C.) through the present day. This is the Heard's major exhibit, **Native People of the Southwest,** and it lets you into a special world illustrated by life-sized Hopi, Navajo and Apache dwellings. The exhibit presents a scholarly and beautiful explanation of the relationship between the environment and Indian culture. For instance, rather than demonstrate how corn is ground, it explains why the Hopis believe the corn is life. This is done through a sensitive blending of art, natural history and anthropological information.

Next visit the **Kachina Gallery** which holds a dazzling display of nearly 1,000 Kachina dolls. These hand-carved, hand-painted wooden figurines represent various Hopi religious spirits. You can trace the progression of this important art form, from old, crudely carved figures to today's slick, sophisticated statues collectors vie for. Be sure to spend time in the museum's art galleries, as well, where different artists are showcased. On your way out, browse through the spacious gift shop. Here you can find fine works by both established and undiscovered Native American artists. After visiting the Heard Museum, you'll know why this facility is the pride of the entire Southwest. Open daily including weekends. Call for hours. Fee. (602) 252-8848.

Squaw Peak Mountain Park. 2701 E. Squaw Peak Dr. Head east on Lincoln Drive to Squaw Peak Drive. Turn left at the light. For a quick desert experience in the heart of the urban scene, drive into Squaw Peak, park and hike. If you have the inclination, join the crowds who religiously trek up and down the well-marked trail to the summit. The park has many ramadas, shelters which offer shady areas for picnicking. Water and restrooms are available. You can call ahead to reserve one of these roofed areas for a large gathering. Since mountain parks are very popular with local residents during the fall, winter and spring, reserved space is often at a premium. Free. (602) 262-4889.

South Mountain Park. 10919 S. Central Ave. Take Central Avenue south to the far end of town, a 15- to 20-minute drive beyond downtown Phoenix. Eventually Central Avenue will curve to the west and you'll approach the park. This more than 13,000-acre mountain range was a gift to the city of Phoenix in the 1920s by a group of far-sighted Phoenix boosters including Claire Booth Luce and Elizabeth Arden. As you enter the park, the ranger at the stone gate house will ask you not to bring any glass containers or alcoholic beverages.

Take a scenic drive up to a mountaintop for a thrilling look down at Phoenix, or park your car and walk the trails. There are many opportunities here for serious biking, walking or hiking. Picnic facilities and restrooms are plentiful. Free. (602) 262-2221.

The Phoenix Zoo. 5810 E. Van Buren Rd. Follow Van Buren east. The facility is located near the border between Phoenix and Scottsdale in Papago Park. One of the largest animal centers in the world in terms of physical size, the Phoenix Zoo presents creatures in their native habitat. Wherever possible, exhibits are appropriately landscaped enclosures instead of cages. Since the zoo area is so large, many people prefer to hop a Zoo Train which winds throughout the grounds regularly. These rides are narrated, and the driver will direct your attention to special points of interest. After the ride, you can walk back along the well-maintained paths to visit your favorite exhibits.

The Phoenix Zoo has a diverse and exotic collection of creatures, and the setting, nestled against the Papago Buttes, is movie-set perfect. There are plentiful well-shaded picnic areas, a snack bar, gift shop and a delightful children's Petting Zoo. Open daily. Fee. (602) 273-7771.

Desert Botanical Garden. 1201 N. Galvin Parkway (next to the Phoenix Zoo in Papago Park). Even those who don't know a desert broom from a grandfather cactus will enjoy the Desert Botanical Garden. After covering the outside gardens, be sure to go inside the greenhouse and see the many kinds of succulents and cacti growing there. Stop at the auditorium where you can study the mounted exhibits and pick up some fascinating botanical facts. Inquire at the visitors center, just inside the front gate, about special events and lectures, many of them free of charge. There's also a book and gift shop on the grounds. Open daily. Fee. (602) 941-1217.

WHERE TO SHOP

Phoenix is a shopper's paradise. The metropolitan area is served by nearly 20 major shopping centers, and there are hundreds of boutiques and stores. If you want to set aside some shopping days, the following two centers are worthy of attention.

Biltmore Fashion Park. 2470 Camelback Rd. The most elegant shopping in Phoenix is found here amid this collection of fine department stores, chic boutiques, restaurants and breezy bricked patios. Even on the hottest summer days, this outdoor shopping area manages to be cool and inviting.

Metrocenter. 9617 Metro Parkway (just west of I-17 between Dunlap and Peoria). An entire "city" on the northwest side, Metrocenter offers 1,600,000 square feet of shopping under a single roof. Once the shopping center went in, an entire mini-city followed. Here you'll find everything you need for visiting or living in Phoenix — from department stores to unique shops to recreation and restaurants.

WHERE TO EAT

Phoenix offers every type of cuisine — from Mongolian and Mexican to Thai and elegant continental. Ask anyone in Phoenix to name a favorite dining spot and you'll get a different answer. Here are a few favorites:

The Duck and Decanter. 622 E. Adams St. in Heritage Square. Place your order, take an outdoor table, and wait to hear your name called. Your sandwich or salad comes in a special "Duck and Decanter" brown bag and no matter what you order, it's great. The albacore tuna on pita bread is a favorite. To satisfy your sweet tooth, the "Duck" always includes a piece of hard candy in the package for dessert. Ask about the special flavor of tea for the day. $-$$; ☐. (602) 253-0759.

Avanti. 2728 E. Thomas Rd. Enter the black and white chic world of Avanti and indulge yourself in Northern Italian continental cuisine. Fish dishes are winners, as well as the pastas and unusual seafood salads. The calamari is outstanding. $$-$$$; ☐. (602) 956-0900.

Arizona Biltmore. 24th Street and Missouri Avenue. There are several restaurants in this resort hotel. For elegance, it's the

Orangerie, considered by many to be the finest establishment in the valley. You can dine and dance in the Gold Room or relax casually at The Adobe Steakhouse. $$-$$$; . (602) 955-6600.

The Golden Eagle. 201 N. Central Ave., at the top of the Valley Bank Center. The views are the best. You'll sit high above the city, with the entire valley spread at your feet. The "Eagle" features continental cuisine. In the summer, ask about specials. $$-$$$; □. (602) 257-7700.

Pointe Tapatio. 11111 N. Seventh St. at the Pointe Tapatio Cliffs Resort. Drive north on Seventh Street to reach this resort, one of The Pointe Resorts which have sprung up throughout the valley. Come here for continental dining and a diverse menu. Ask to be seated on the patio so you can enjoy the star-studded sky. $$-$$$; □. (602) 866-7500.

Willy & Guillermo's. 5600 N. Central Ave. This sprawling hacienda-style restaurant offers "gringo" Mexican food and plenty of it. Be sure to read the menu. It's crazy and fun. The "Enchilada Seafooda" (their spelling!) is great. $-$$; □. (602) 266-1900.

Rustler's Rooste. 7777 Pointe Parkway at South Mountain. (That silent "e" on "Rooste" tells you that this is one of The Pointe's resort centers.) There's a slide for those who choose to use it which deposits you into the restaurant. The specialty here is hearty Western fare, especially barbecued items. It's all a mite corny, but it's a good place to see city lights twinkling over the desert. $$; □. (602) 231-9111.

Day Trips
From Flagstaff

With Flagstaff as your base (see DAY TRIP 4, NORTH FROM PHOENIX), the entire northern third of Arizona is open to you. You'll see wonders of the ancient world such as the Grand Canyon, the quiet beauty of lakes and forests, and remote Indian villages whose inhabitants live very much as their ancestors did hundreds of years ago.

As you plan your trips, remember that northern Arizona is different from the southern and central sections of the state. During the winter, snowstorms can rush in quickly, covering the highways and turning an easy drive into a nightmare. If you're planning a visit during the fall, winter or early spring, phone ahead to check the weather.

In summer, temperatures around Flagstaff remain moderate, with warm days and cool evenings. But as you travel into the high desert areas of the northeastern section of the state or to the far western border near California, you're back in the sizzling heat. In these areas, don't forget to carry water in your car and be prepared for high temperatures.

The following trips are planned to include a maximum amount of sightseeing in a minimum of time. For Northern Arizona, stretch your time limit for a day trip from two to four or even five driving hours one way. Many of these trips are better done in tandem — doing one trip one day and picking up the following trip the next day without heading back to Flagstaff. Combining trips cuts the driving distance and lets you maximize out-of-the-car time.

However, if you don't have a weekend or can't string a couple of days together, relax. You can make each of these a separate overnight experience as long as you're prepared to go the distance to get back to Flagstaff.

One last piece of advice. This vast area is sparsely inhabited. You are wise to carry some food in the car, as well as water, soft drinks or juice. Clean, well-equipped rest stops are often few and far between, so when you see a decent-looking gas station, you should stop if your tank is below two-thirds full or somebody needs to use a restroom. Often you won't see another gas station for miles. Forewarned, you shouldn't get caught in the wilds.

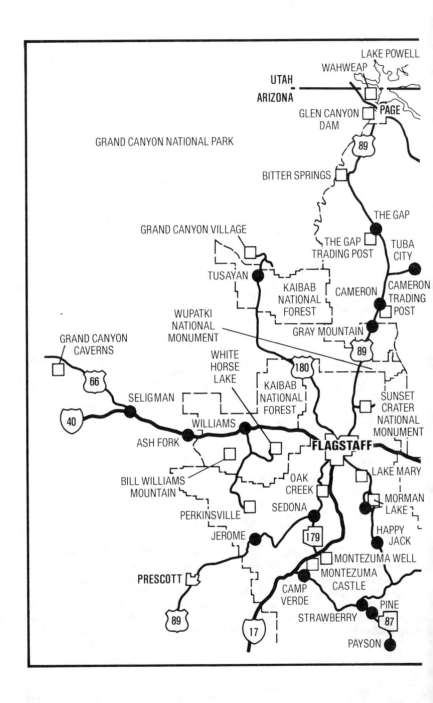

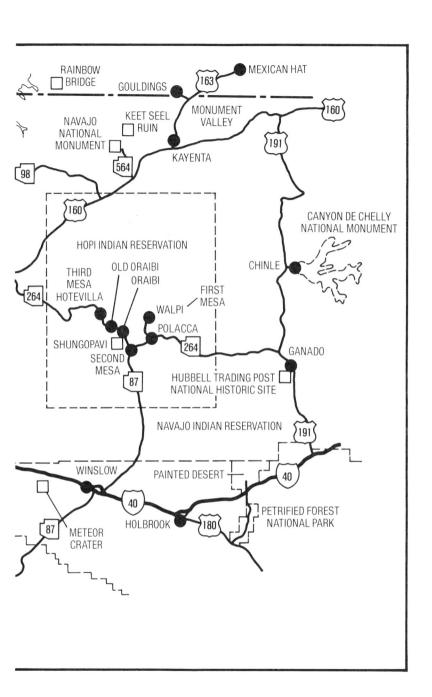

Day Trip 1

SUNSET CRATER AND
WUPATKI NATIONAL MONUMENT
PAGE AND GLEN CANYON DAM
LAKE POWELL
NAVAJO NATIONAL MONUMENT

SUNSET CRATER AND WUPATKI NATIONAL MONUMENT

Follow US-89 north from Flagstaff approximately 19 miles. Turn right on the road to Sunset Crater and follow it two miles to the visitors center. A Loop Road takes you to Wupatki Indian ruins. Continue on the Loop Road to US-89 and turn left to return to Flagstaff. Wind through the volcanic region northeast of Flagstaff and circle through Sunset Crater and the Wupatki Indian ruins, 25 miles from Flagstaff. To better grasp the geological and archeological implications of the area, stop at the visitors centers at both Sunset Crater, a 1000-foot-high volcanic cone, and Wupatki, which offers 35,000 acres of prehistoric Indian ruins. Even nonscientific types love the famous Wupatki ball court. Open daily. Free. For more information about these attractions, call Sunset Crater National Monument, (602) 527-7042, and Wupatki National Monument, (602) 527-7040.

PAGE AND GLEN CANYON DAM

Time permitting, continue north on US-89 to cover Page and Lake Powell. Stay overnight in Page, then go on to Navajo National Monument the next morning and pick up the Northeast day trip at Kayenta. Taking two days to see Lake Powell and Navajo National Monument allows ample time to explore. Visit Page, Lake Powell, and tour Navajo National Monument. If you have only one day to cover this, you'll drive through Page, see Lake Powell from the shore, and take a fast trip to the Navajo National Monument. But cramming all this into one day will leave you hungry for more.

As you proceed north on US-89 from Flagstaff, you'll pass the tiny hamlet of **Gray Mountain.** Here you enter the vast expanse of the Navajo Indian Reservation. Summer travelers need to move their watches ahead one hour: while Arizona doesn't observe daylight saving time, the Navajo Nation does. This time change can be confusing and even frustrating if you aren't forewarned. You don't want to plan to arrive somewhere by 5 p.m. only to find that it's 6 p.m. and you've missed what you want to see.

Eight miles north of Gray Mountain on US-89, you'll see the **Cameron Trading Post,** the first of a number of Indian trading posts in this region. Cameron is actually a complex of buildings made of lovely native stone and wood. Here you'll discover a treasure trove of items — some exquisite, others tourist trinkets. There's also food service which isn't fancy but is adequate if you're hungry or thirsty.

After leaving Cameron, the highway crosses the Little Colorado River, one of the major tributaries of the Colorado River. Another 31 miles up the road you'll come to a second famous trading post, **The Gap.** Both Cameron and The Gap played important roles in opening the Arizona Territory. Trading posts helped to establish an economy which benefited both the white and Indian societies. To today's casual observer these places appear to be scenic tourist stops, but they aren't. Years ago trading posts were lifelines for the Indians and traders who depended upon them. The Indians traded rugs, jewelry and other hand-crafted items for groceries and needed supplies. Occasionally, a Navajo man or woman would pawn a prized piece of jewelry for money and the trader would keep the item until the owner could redeem it. Some owners never were able to get their heirlooms back and "pawn jewelry," cherished by collectors, eventually was sold.

With a full day facing you, unless you need to stop, push on and explore these posts another day. Page and the wonders of Lake Powell await.

At Bitter Springs US-89 bends east. Continue on US-89 to Page. Like all towns built to support generating plants, this community owes its life to power and glory — the power of Glen Canyon Dam and the glory of the Grand Canyon. The dam was built in the 1950s; the Canyon has been under construction for millions and millions of years.

Glen Canyon Dam was constructed at a cost of $260 million, a hefty sum, especially when you consider that to replace that plant today would cost $800 million. It was October 15, 1956, when President Dwight D. Eisenhower pushed a button on his desk in the White House 2100 miles away to set off the first blast. Four years later, June 17, 1960, the last 4,901,000 cubic yards of concrete were poured. The resulting dam, a 583-foot high wall, holds back the second largest man-made lake in North America. (Lake Mead, also formed by the Colorado River, is the largest.) Glen Canyon conserves water from a 246,000-square-mile watershed, provides electricity for the Pacific Southwest and the Rocky Mountain areas, and gives Page a reason for being.

A small, friendly community dedicated to tourism and electricity, Page was first staked out as a temporary government construction camp in 1957. It was named for the first commissioner of the Reclamation Service established under President Theodore Roosevelt. Since then, the town has thrived. There's a busy airport, visitor center, museum, library, and 11 churches side by side on just one street. (Two other churches are located elsewhere in town.)

Near Page, US-89 climbs, and you'll get your first view of Glen Canyon Dam below. Behind it, the magical blue world of Lake Powell spreads out, improbably set into the rocky abyss of this far-eastern section of the Grand Canyon. Lake Powell is renowned throughout the world for its astonishing beauty, and no tourist yet has been disappointed by the views.

WHERE TO GO

Glen Canyon Dam and Carl Hayden Visitor Center. On US-89. This is a highly recommended stop. In the visitors center, an illustrated history depicts the construction and use of the dam. If you have time, watch the audiovisual program. If not, at least browse through the easy-to-follow displays which reveal fascinating details about the dam. You can easily spend 30 minutes in the Carl Hayden Visitor Center. If you have time, take the guided tour of the generating plant given almost every hour. Visitors are taken from the crest of the dam down one of three elevators into the power plant where they can see the inner workings of the turbines and understand how this dam delivers power to much of the western United States. Nearly an hour in length, the tour is not strenuous; you'll walk about a third of a mile. It's a cool 50° F. down under, so bring a wrap. Open daily. Free. (602) 645-2511.

The Page Visitor Center/Museum. 6 Lake Powell Blvd. Continue north on US-89 until you see a sign for the Business District of Page. Follow the signs. Drive over the bridge and take Lake Shore Boulevard to the Chamber of Commerce and Visitor Center and Museum, all located in one building. Check with the visitor center for additional information on the area, and then take a quick trip through the museum, which is filled with artifacts and memorabilia commemorating John Wesley Powell and his expeditions.

Major Powell is acknowledged as the first explorer of the Colorado River and the Grand Canyon. A Civil War veteran, he lost his right arm at Shiloh before setting out on this expedition. The 35-year old adventurer first conquered the Colorado in 1869, setting in at Green River, Wyoming. He went back in 1871 and did the trip again. Thanks to his meticulous personal journal, generations of "river rats" (people who run the rapids in the Grand Canyon) and canyon and river enthusiasts relive his experiences and can identify with his thought-provoking impressions. Open daily. Free. (602) 645-2741.

Wahweap Lodge and Marina. 4.5 miles from Glen Canyon Dam on US-89 northwest of Page. Turn right at the sign for the marina (the only way you can turn) onto a paved road which leads to Wahweap. One of four marinas on Lake Powell, Wahweap (pronounced Waa'-weep) is the most accessible for tourists. Here you'll find overnight accommodations, fine dining, a gift shop and a host of tours and adventures. Even if you don't plan to spend the night or eat at Wahweap, you'll want to stroll through the lodge to lose yourself in the views of the lake. Lake Powell is a complete recreational wonderland — the fishing is great. The views better. And the deep, cool blue water and out-of-the-way beaches the best. Other lakes in Arizona may be closer to major cities or have more sandy beaches, but only Lake Powell, with its fjords and inlets, scallops and gulleys, and wrapped in a golden desert sun, comes so close to perfection.

WHAT TO DO

There's so much to do in this area that you can spend a week or an entire season at Lake Powell. All of the trips listed below depart from Wahweap. Even if you can only squeeze in a two-hour excursion, do so. You'll *see* the lake from the shore, but you can only *experience* its mystic setting when you're on it and surrounded by its sandy, sculpted mountains. To make reservations for boat tours or accommodations, or to inquire about adventures in the area, contact Del E. Webb Recreational Properties, Box 29040, Phoenix, AZ 85038, or call 1-800-528-6154 toll free or (602) 278-8888 if calling from Phoenix.

Here is a sampling of the cruises you can take on the lake:

The Canyon King. Make arrangements at Wahweap Lodge and Marina, where the boats depart. Treat yourself to a ride on the only genuine paddle wheeler operating west of the Rockies, or enhance this experience with a sunset/moonlight dinner cruise. The Canyon King ferries 150 guests at a time and operates all year. You also can make special arrangements for large groups or parties through Del E. Webb Recreational Properties, Box 29040, Phoenix, AZ 85038. Fee. (602) 645-2433.

All Day and Half-Day Rainbow Bridge Tour. Both tours leave from

Wahweap Marina. The half-day involves a five-hour trip; the all day allows for more side channel cruising. You'll depart Wahweap in the early morning and follow the main channel of Lake Powell to Rainbow Bridge. This natural wonder literally fills the sky as you approach the docking area. You can read the dimensions but the size of the stone arch will still astound you. The dome of the United States Capitol building could fit underneath it. After your boat docks, there's a short hike to get to the base of the bridge. Be sure to read the inspiring commemorative plaque.

Glen Canyon Dam was built over strong environmental objections. People grieved over the flooding of Glen Canyon which John Welsey Powell considered one of the most beautiful areas in the Grand Canyon. They feared what traffic would do to fragile places like Rainbow Bridge. The dam did doom the canyon to a watery death, but the trade-off was Lake Powell, a shimmering body of water which dances between the intricate, spidery spires and rolling sandstone mountaintops. Neither the water nor the exposed desert canyon seems aware of the other's presence. You'll see the two worlds of sea and land meeting but not merging.

Since the dam was built and Lake Powell formed, more people see Rainbow Bridge each month than had ever seen it collectively in its history, before the dam was built. But so far, visitors are considerate and the area surrounding the bridge appears to be surviving well. Fee. For more information contact Del E. Webb Recreational Properties, Box 29040, Phoenix, AZ 85038. (602) 645-2433.

The Navajo Tapestry Cruise. This short excursion on Lake Powell (two and one-half hours) gives travelers a fast but true flavor of this wonderland. You leave from Wahweap Lodge and the boat glides between the walls of Antelope Canyon, cruises Navajo Canyon (from which the cruise takes its name), and then returns via Antelope Island, Warm Creek and Castle Rock Strait. This is a brief, but intensely satisfying way to see Lake Powell. Fee. Contact Del E. Webb Recreational Properties, Box 29040, Phoenix, AZ 85038. (602) 645-2433.

Houseboating. Enjoy the water for a couple of days and nights or stay a week on a well-equipped, luxurious floating house. The best speeds for a houseboat are "slow" and "stopped," so wise houseboaters dock their boats at secluded coves early on and use a speedboat to water ski and explore the thousands of skinny little canyons that lead from the main body of the lake. With 1900 miles of shoreline to choose from, you can houseboat on Lake Powell repeatedly and never explore the same spot twice. Be prepared to get lost on Lake Powell. Most first-timers do, but keep reading your maps and you'll come out fine. During the height of the summer season, you'll need to reserve a houseboat far in advance. This is an ideal family experience. For price information and availability, contact Del E. Webb Recreational Properties, Box 29040, Phoenix, AZ 85038. Fee. (602) 645-2433.

Colorado River Float. Departs from the Page Museum, 6 Lake Powell Blvd. For would-be river runners who don't like white-water ·

craziness, a float trip provides the ideal alternative. You'll float for a day through the polished splendor of Marble Canyon, stop for lunch on the bank, and see ancient petroglyphs from the canyon floor. After the 15-mile float trip, you'll feel as if you've "done" the Colorado. This is great fun for families with young children and anyone who wants to see the Grand Canyon the most scenic way — from the bottom up. Fee. Inquire about float trips by calling (800) 528-6154, (602) 278-8888 or (602) 645-3279 at Wahweap.

WHERE TO EAT

Wahweap Lodge. Wahweap Marina, Lake Powell. The main dining room has a dazzling view of the lake. At night the room shimmers with elegance and by day you can gaze out on the blue expanse. The specialty is prime rib, but the menu is varied and well-prepared. Ask about the daily specials. $$; □. (602) 645-2433.

WHERE TO STAY

Wahweap Lodge. Wahweap Marina, Lake Powell. The rooms are large and spacious, but if you aren't on the ground floor, be prepared to tote your own luggage up the stairs. You can reserve rooms at the Lake Powell Motel, get a housekeeping unit or rent space for a camper or RV through the central reservation service. Contact Del E. Webb Recreational Properties, Box 29040, Phoenix, AZ 85038, or call 1-800-528-6154 or (602) 278-8888.

The Holiday Inn. 287 North Lake Powell Blvd. in Page. This is right up the street from the Page Chamber of Commerce / visitors center / museum building. Although not on the lake, the motel units are quite nice. Call (602) 645-8851.

NAVAJO NATIONAL MONUMENT

When you're ready to push on another 88 miles, leave Lake Powell and drive southeast on A-98 for 66 miles to US-160. At the junction, head northeast on US-160 toward Kayenta. Twelve miles further, you'll see a sign for A-564. Turn left and follow it north for nine miles.

This drive will take about two hours during which time you'll cross the Navajo Indian Reservation, an often desolate landscape. Watch for the Navajo hogans, low, round houses which many Navajo families still use as homes. The hogan doorway will always face east, where the sun rises. When you reach A-564, you'll be on a paved road leading to Navajo National Monument. This is a collection of three wonderfully preserved Indian ruins: all that is left of pre-Columbian communities known as Keet Seel; Betatakin (pronounced Be-tah-tah-kin); and Inscription House. Remote enough to be off the beaten tourist track, and romantic, these ruins provide an unusually personal look into the past for travelers who have the stamina and time to go the distance.

As is recommended for all national parks and monuments, your first stop should be the visitors center. Here you'll get your bearings. Although this is called the Navajo National Monument, the name refers to its location on the Navajo Reservation. The remnants of dwellings here are from the Anasazi civilization, a pre-Columbian people who inhabited this area around 1200 B.C. The exhibits and the slide program at the center describe the life and times of Anasazi. You'll learn about their homes and crops and also get a quick lesson in the geology of this area. For more information on Navajo National Monument, write HC 71, Box 3, Tonalea, AZ 86044-9704. Open daily year round. Free. (602) 672-2366.

WHERE TO GO

Betatakin. Guided tours are available to this Anasazi cliff dwelling throughout the year. Take an easy walk along Sandal Trail, which leads to an overlook of Betatakin. As you peer into this ruin, you'll sense that these people have left only momentarily and are due to return soon. During the season, June 1 to mid-September, there are three daily tours. After September, there is just one tour a day scheduled.

Betatakin means "house on a ledge," and this cluster of dwellings is literally set onto a massive cavern in the canyon wall. The most accessible of the ruins here, Betatakin was constructed and abandoned in two generations between 1250 B.C. and 1300 B.C. The 135 rooms constituted a total community. There's a kiva, or ceremonial chamber, granaries, and living quarters.

Discovered in 1909 by Byron Cummings, a pioneer archeologist of the Southwest, and John Wetherill, a rancher and trader, Betatakin was made safe for exploration in 1917 by Neil M. Judd of the Smithsonian Institution. The one-mile round-trip walk from the visitors center takes about an hour. Bring binoculars to see these dwellings from the vantage of the rim. Ranger-guided tours, which descend into the ruin, are limited to 20 people at a time because of the fragility of the area. These excursions take about three hours and involve some strenuous climbing. The canyon is 700 feet deep, equal to a 70-story building, and the altitude is 7200 feet, which can be tiring for anyone, even those who are physically fit. Anyone with a heart condition should not attempt this climb. Free.

Inscription House. As of this printing tours are no longer available. The site is closed for stabilization to make it safe and to prevent erosion under the stress of future exploration and tours.

Keet Seel. Tucked away in a remote canyon eight miles from the visitors center, Keet Seel is the largest cliff dwelling in the state and can only be reached on foot or on horseback. Either way, it's a strenuous trip but the journey is well worth the trouble for people who have adventurous hearts, strong legs and iron seats.

You must make arrangements for this trip with a ranger ahead of time, because visits to Keet Seel are limited to 20 tourists a day. A Navajo family leads tours on horseback to Keet Seel, and if you are up for this rugged trip, be ready for some rough riding. The horses have two speeds: walk and wild gallop. True, you'll take a ride on the wild side, but when you reach Keet Seel, you'll forget your soreness and marvel at this extraordinarily well-preserved Anasazi ruin. Make arrangements for this experience at the visitors center. Fee for renting the horses.

From Navajo National Monument you can head south on A-564 to US-160, then south on US-160 to US-89, and US-89 south back to Flagstaff. Or, you can return to Page for the night.

Day Trip 1

KAYENTA
MONUMENT VALLEY, UTAH

KAYENTA

Kayenta is located 150 miles northeast of Flagstaff and the trip takes about three hours. Go north on US-89 to its junction with US-160 and continue northeast on US-160 to Kayenta. This is a tiny town by American standards, but it is a major community on the Navajo Reservation. Kayenta is the jumping-off point for Monument Valley, your next destination. From Kayenta, turn north on US-163 to Monument Valley and Mexican Hat.

WHERE TO EAT

The Golden Sands Cafe. On US-163 one mile north of the Kayenta Holiday Inn. Feast on the Golden Sands Navajo taco, a delectable combination of chili and Navajo fry bread. You can choose from three sizes of tacos. The place is a favorite of locals and tourists, and there is usually a collection of pickup trucks in the parking lot. The portions are huge, the prices reasonable, and the atmosphere is authentic Navajo Indian Reservation. $; □. (602) 697-3550.

WHERE TO STAY

The Holiday Inn, Kayenta. At the junction of US-160 and US-163. You'll find clean, adequate accommodations. Nothing fancy, but considering the remote location, this Holiday Inn offers a surprisingly nice option for travelers. There's even a swimming pool. $$. □. (602) 697-3221.

MONUMENT VALLEY, UTAH

From Kayenta, take US-163 north approximately 20 miles. At a crossroads just over the Utah state line, bear right to the Monument Valley Visitors Center. If Salvadore Dali had sculpted a landscape, this would be it. Stark spires rise abruptly from the sandy floor, and the rocky formations appear to have been dropped onto the flat earth, as if some ancient people flew in from the stars, deposited their rocky cargo, and disappeared.

Monument Valley is not a national park but, rather, a Navajo tribal park consisting of 29,816 acres owned and managed by the Navajo Tribal Council. The valley was made famous by John Wayne, who starred in many classic westerns which were filmed here.

At the visitors center, you'll see a sign pointing to a 17-mile unpaved scenic loop through the park. You can pick up a brochure inside which describes a self-guided tour. Along the way there are 11 numbered scenic stops. Although the signs say you can drive your car on this road, think twice before you do so. The road is narrow, rutted and banked by deep sands. In short, it isn't terrific. Most people prefer to take a guided jeep tour, especially since many of the more spectacular rock formations can be seen only from off the road.

During the summer season, expect high daytime temperatures and long lines to get into the visitors center or the park. But know that it's well worth any inconvenience. In the winter, Monument Valley is often closed because of snow. Open daily, weather permitting. Fee. (602) 727-3287.

WHERE TO EAT AND STAY

Gouldings. Six miles west of the visitors center just over the Utah state line off US-163. As you approach Monument Valley, you'll see a cluster of reddish-colored buildings built into the cliff to your left. Gouldings Trading Post complex is a wonderful blend of nostalgia and convenience.

Meals are served family style, and a dinner bell rings to announce breakfast, lunch or dinner. You can eat here even if you aren't a guest, but check for dining hours. Your waitresses will be Navajo women in native dress. Because this is a favorite stop for international tours, you're apt to hear a multitude of languages spoken at any meal. Order from a menu that features Navajo home cooking or American food.

The accommodations are rustic, but delightful, and offer incomparable views of Monument Valley. You'll need reservations in advance to get into this popular spot. Gouldings is open from mid-March through mid-October. The staff will arrange for tours of Monument Valley with native guides. $$; □. (801) 727-3231.

From here you can retrace your steps to Flagstaff or pick up DAY TRIP 2, NORTHEAST FROM FLAGSTAFF. If you have more time combining these two trips can be a marvelous four- to seven-day vacation.

Day Trip 2

CANYON DE CHELLY NATIONAL MONUMENT
GANADO AND THE HUBBELL TRADING POST

CANYON DE CHELLY NATIONAL MONUMENT

Canyon Chelly Monument is approximately 80 miles southeast of Monument Valley on Indian Route 64. From Monument Valley, drive south on US-163 to Kayenta. At the junction of US-160 and 163, drive east on US-160 about 40 miles to where US-160 meets US-191. Go south on US-191 for 75 miles to Chinle and the entrance to Canyon de Chelly (pronounced "de Shay"). To see Canyon de Chelly properly requires at least one overnight if you are coming from Monument Valley and two if Flagstaff is your base.

Canyon de Chelly is quite unlike Monument Valley. Where Monument Valley is stark and golden desert, Canyon de Chelly is pink and warm. It is one of the most appealing of Arizona's canyons. As you enter the canyon on Indian Route 64, you will see the visitors center directly ahead of you.

This park boasts towering sculpted rock formations, sheer and colorful cliffs, and picture-postcard scenery. It is inhabited both by modern-day Indians and memories of ancient ones. The Pueblo Indians, who vanished from this area around 1350 A.D., abandoned their dwellings forever. Their spirit infuses the ruins within the canyon walls. Hundreds of ancient communities, many of them poised on sandstone ledges within colorful caverns, give witness to the earlier vitality of this place.

The Navajos arrived in the area sometime before the 18th century. Even today a small enclave of Navajo families lives in modern dwellings on the canyon floor, tends sheep and grows crops.

WHERE TO GO

Self-guided tours. Pick up brochures describing these tours at the Canyon de Chelly Visitor Center. When walking or driving on the rim, be sure to obey all signs. In places, it's a dizzying 400 foot drop onto the canyon floor.

Guided jeep tours. To fully appreciate the geology, history and anthropology of this exquisite canyon, take a guided half-day or full-day jeep tour. Make arrangements at the Thunderbird Lodge, P. O. Box 548, Chinle, AZ 86503. Unless you have an extensive interest in ancient Indian civilization, the half-day trip is your best bet; a full day could leave you exhausted. In summer, as you bounce along the canyon floor in an open jeep, you may need the protection of sunscreen and a hat. You may even want to take a canteen or thermos with water. Open daily. Fee. ⊔. (602) 674-5443 or (602) 674-5263.

WHERE TO EAT

Thunderbird Lodge Motel. On US-191. The food tends to be heavy and starchy but it's prepared and served by a Navajo staff in a charming building, circa 1896, which was the original trading post. The only dining establishment in the immediate area of the canyon, this *is* your only choice. Open daily during breakfast, lunch and dinner hours. $; □. (602) 674-5443 or (602) 674-5263.

WHERE TO STAY

Thunderbird Lodge Motel. On US-191. This historic lodge offers the most complete facilities in Navajoland. The rooms are clean and moderately priced, and the location, at the mouth of the canyon, is magnificent. You'll find a gift shop to browse through and you can make arrangements for tours right at the lodge. Make sure you bring a light jacket or sweater for summer evenings if you visit from April to November. In the winter, you'll need to bundle up. For information, write to Thunderbird Lodge Motel, P. O. Box 548, Chinle, AZ 86503. $$; □. (602) 674-5443 or (602) 674-5263.

Canyon de Chelly Motel. As you enter Chinle, south on US-191, turn left at the intersection — the only one in town. Don't depend upon road signs in this area. Often, if the road is under repair, the signs come down. (Take solace in the fact that Chinle is tiny and you really cannot get lost.) $$; □. (602) 674-5288.

GANADO AND THE HUBBELL TRADING POST

Hubbell Trading Post National Historic Site. One mile west of Ganado. Before returning to Flagstaff from Canyon de Chelly, you can continue south 30 miles on US-191 to the intersection of A-264, then five miles east to Ganado and the Hubbell Trading Post National Historic Site. A national treasure, the trading post is worth the visit.

The rug room at the Hubbell Trading Post rivals any museum collection in the world. If you're in the market for a Navajo rug, this is an ideal place to shop. The knowledgeable salespeople will be happy to tell you about the patterns and weavers. The only modern-day touch is that, along with the name of the weaver, you'll also occasionally find a polaroid photograph of the weaver attached to the ticket. You also can browse through exquisite jewelry, sandpaintings, books and trinkets or even pick up food supplies if you plan to camp in the area. Groceries are sold in the front room.

John Lorenzo Hubbell was the dean of traders for the Navajos, and his trading post continues to act as a bridge between the Indian and Anglo worlds. In its heyday, the post offered a place for Navajos to socialize as well as to conduct business. VIPs of every culture who passed through northeastern Arizona during the late 1800s and early 1900s stopped here. The guest list includes presidents, generals, writers, scientists and artists.

Today business continues as usual in this elegant pocket of the state. The atmosphere hasn't changed; Navajos and tourists still come by to trade and talk.

Hubbell's career spanned critical years for the Navajos. When he came to the territory to open his trading post, the Indians were adjusting to life on a reservation and were attempting to cope with the restrictions placed upon them by the United States government. Hubbell offered his friendship when great numbers of Navajo were struggling to free themselves from the confines of Fort Sumner in New Mexico. He sympathized with the Navajo and often spoke out on their behalf. When he died in 1930, one of Hubbell's native friends eulogized him at the memorial service saying:

> *"You wear out your shoes, you buy another pair;*
> *When the food is gone, you buy more;*
> *You gather melons, and more will grow on the vine;*
> *You grind your corn and make bread which you eat;*
> *And next year you have plenty more corn.*
> *But my friend Don Lorenzo is gone,*
> *and none to take his place."*

After browsing through the trading post, walk around the grounds and see the Hubbell home. Open daily. Free. (602) 755-3254.

From Ganado, there are several ways to return to Flagstaff. The fastest route is US-191 south to I-40. Then head west on I-40 to Flagstaff. Another alternative is to take A-264 west to A-87, turn south on A-87, and then west on I-40 to Flagstaff. Get some sleep at Canyon de Chelly if you plan to head west on A-264 to Polacca for DAY TRIP 3, NORTHEAST FROM FLAGSTAFF, after visiting Ganado.

Day Trip 3

INDIAN COUNTRY:
FIRST, SECOND AND THIRD MESAS

This is a wonderful trip which shouldn't be rushed. Because of the great distances in this part of the state, visiting more remote areas means stretching your usual day trip time limit.

As you plan, consider that the Hopi Reservation roads found in this sector are often narrow, two-lane byways. You won't make fast time, so add another hour to your excursion limit.

You can begin the trip in Flagstaff, heading east on I-40 to Winslow and picking up the turn-off for A-87 north three miles east of there. Follow A-87 north for 65 miles to Second Mesa on the Hopi Indian Reservation, then turn right (east) for seven miles and actually start at Polacca on First Mesa.

A better option might be to combine this trip with Day Trip Two previously described. Time permitting, you will enjoy this journey more if you can begin it refreshed after a good night's sleep at Canyon de Chelly. After driving 30 miles south to Ganado and stopping at the Hubbell Trading Post (see DAY TRIP 2, NORTHEAST FROM FLAGSTAFF), head west on A-264 to Polacca.

If you look at a map, you'll see that the Hopi (pronounced Ho'-pee) nation is plunked down in the middle of the vast Navajo reservation. Although they live in close proximity, the Hopi and the Navajo couldn't be more different. Historically the Hopi, whose ancestors are the Anasazi, have been pueblo dwellers — homebodies content to build permanent villages and cement family ties. The Navajo, in contrast, are nomadic farmers and sheepherders. In fact, the word "Hopi" means "the peaceful ones," and traditionally these people have led a peaceful, agrarian life.

The windswept mesas of the Hopi reservation have long been a source of inspiration to the Hopi and non-Indians alike. As you drive through this reservation on A-264, you'll feel a subtle pull, the magic which

143

makes life in the fast track seem ridiculous. At first, the landscape seems barren, but look again. Everywhere you will see corn growing, even in the most improbable corners of backyards and in the rockiest soil. To the Hopi, corn represents life, and they cherish this food for its nutritional and spiritual values.

If this is your first trip to the Hopi Reservation, or Hopi, as it is more commonly called, you may wonder where the ancient villages are. Etched against the horizon, high on flattened mountain tops, the tiny pueblos jut against the sky like jack-o-lantern teeth. Although the Hopi have lived here for hundreds of years, they do not intrude upon Mother Earth. They live gently and inconspicuously, coaxing life from this rocky soil they call their land.

All but one of the villages you may visit are located on or near the areas called First, Second and Third Mesas. The names refer to the chronological shift of the Hopi population from 1500 A.D. to 1900 A.D. First the Hopis settled in Walpi, (the area now known as First Mesa), and they gradually moved westward to Oraibi and Hotevilla. However, since they are descendants of the Anasazi culture, there's evidence that ancestors of the Hopi occupied this area for over 2000 years.

Life goes on here, in many instances as it always has, with families living in ancient pueblo dwellings high on treeless cliffs. Some villagers have moved down from the mesa, spending most of the year in modern, government-built housing at the foot of the mountains. These Hopi go back to the old village only for festivals and holidays.

During the year, Hopi dances are frequently held on the mesas. These ceremonies are often open to the public. To inquire when public dances are scheduled call the Hopi Cultural Center at (602) 734-2401. If you decide to plan a visit during a dance, understand that the Hopi do not share our Anglo clock fetish. Dances begin when they begin — no sooner, no later. They end when they are over. This can be one hour or six hours. Indians have a totally different concept of time. Bring patience, a chair, and a warm blanket or heavy jacket. Above all, *do not* bring cameras. Picture taking is *not* allowed during dances.

The Snake Dance, held in late August, is one of the most spectacular Hopi ceremonies that visitors are allowed to see. Many of the other tribal dances involve Hopi men dressed up to symbolize various Kachinas (Hopi gods), but the Snake Dance does not involve Kachinas. Instead, men dance with live bullsnakes, gartersnakes and rattlesnakes in their mouths invoking the gods to send needed rain for the crops.

WHERE TO GO

Walpi, First Mesa. All the ancient villages are off the main roads, situated high atop the mesas. In the past, a mountaintop location protected the village from intruders.

As you drive through the reservation on A-264, you'll see signs pointing to Polacca, an Indian village. At Polacca, you'll spot a gravel road that leads north to Walpi. (There are no names on the few streets leading to these ancient villages.) The narrow road climbs and makes several sharp turns. Although the pueblo buildings may appear to be closing in on you, don't worry. This road is fine for passenger car travel. Once on top of the mesa, park and walk around. You'll see the ancient plaza, still used for ceremonials with its kiva (underground ceremonial chamber) near the center. While you may freely explore the plaza and old pueblo dwellings, the kiva is off-limits.

Walpi is an especially picturesque village which comes to life during important ceremonies. You will find that the Hopi who live here are extremely friendly and you may be invited inside some homes to see hand-crafted art items. If you are interested in native arts, by all means, accept the invitations.

Don't take Hopi hospitality for granted. Observe all the signs posted in the ancient villages that ask you not to take any photographs, make sketches, or make any sound recordings. Remember: when you are in Hopi (or any other reservation), you are a guest in another country.

When you leave First Mesa, continue west on A-264 and you'll see signs leading to Shipolovi (Shi-pah'-lo-vee) and Shongopovi (Shun-go'-pa-vee), other well-known old villages on Second Mesa. You may either visit or see them from a distance. Continue toward Oraibi. Soon you'll see the Hopi Cultural Center, a cluster of psuedo-pueblos, on your right. If you're hungry, thirsty or tired of driving, this is a good place to stop. You'll find a restaurant, gift shop, small museum and overnight accommodations here.

Oraibi, Third Mesa. From the cultural center, continue west on A-264 to Oraibi. You may want to take a quick trip to Old Oraibi. Like Walpi, this community hovers on a high, narrow, rocky ledge. The road to Old Oraibi heads off to your left (south) shortly after you pass Oraibi (sometimes called "New Oraibi"). Although parts of the settlement are in ruins, the village is very much a part of modern Hopi life. When you're finished visiting here, drive west on A-264 toward Hotevilla.

Hotevilla, Third Mesa (Charles Loloma's studio). As you drive west toward Hotevilla on A-264, watch for a house off by itself set back from the road on the left (or south) side of the highway. The building has stained-glass windows, a true rarity for Hopi. A twisted, gnarled tree sits in the front yard. There is no sign pointing the way, but if you have any doubt, ask anyone the way to "Charles' studio."

This is the studio and Hopi home of Charles Loloma, the artist and jeweler who single-handedly changed the look of Indian jewelry in the mid-1960s. Before Loloma, Indian craftsmen fashioned rings, bracelets, belts and necklaces from silver, turquoise and coral. Loloma introduced colored stones, like lapis, malachite, shell and ironwood, and wrapped them in gold. He reshaped the old designs and breathed new life into this art. Indian jewelry hasn't been the same since. The Loloma style, although often imitated, remains distinctive. Loloma is a colorful personality, sometimes called the "Louis Tiffany" of Indian jewelry. A practicing Hopi who dances in the Snake Dance, he loves expensive cars and owns his own plane which his pilot flies from the airstrip Charles laughingly calls "Hopi International." His costly work is prized by collectors throughout the world who cherish the innovation of a true "Loloma" design.

Charles does not publish his telephone number. The best way to meet him is to write ahead: Charles Loloma, P. O. Box 185, Hotevilla, AZ 86030, and request an appointment. If the artist is available, he'll be delighted to give you a personal tour of his studio and tell you about his work. If you are in Scottsdale, you can see a dazzling display of Loloma designs at The Lovena Ohl Gallery (see SCOTTSDALE, DAY TRIP 1 EAST FROM PHOENIX).

From Hotevilla, return to the Hopi Cultural Center, if that's where you plan to dine or stay, or continue northwest on A-264 to the junction of US-160, turn west to US-89, and head south into Flagstaff.

WHERE TO EAT AND STAY

The Hopi Cultural Center. On A-264, five miles west of the junction with A-87. The dining room is big and airy and you'll be served by Hopi women in native dress. Order the Hopi specialties: Hopi stew made with chunks of lamb and anything made with blue corn, a special type of corn grown and used here. $-$$; □.

If you plan to spend the night, call ahead for reservations and be prepared to rough it some. You will not find the same quality of service and accommodations on the reservation as you'll find in the cities, but unless you are pulling a camper or driving an RV, this is your only choice for an overnight stay. $$; □. (602) 734-2401.

Day Trip 1

METEOR CRATER
PAINTED DESERT
PETRIFIED FOREST

METEOR CRATER

Leaving Flagstaff, drive east on I-40 toward Winslow. Twenty miles before you reach Winslow, you'll see an exit for Meteor Crater. Head south on the well-marked, paved road to this fascinating natural site.

Meteor Crater was formed in 20,000 B.C. when a meteoric mass, traveling 33,000 miles per hour from interplanetary space, struck earth. The impact, blowing nearly a half-billion tons of rock from the surface, destroyed all plant and animal life within 100 miles. In contemporary times this perfectly preserved, huge hole in the ground has tantalized scientists who use it as a living laboratory. Meteor Crater hit the news when the Apollo astronauts used it as a practice surface to train for their lunar walk. Discovered in 1871, the crater has impressive statistics. It measures 4150 feet from rim to rim, is more than three miles in circumference, and is 570 feet deep. In addition to staring at the crater, you can visit the Museum of Astrogeology, the Astronaut Hall of Fame, and well-appointed gift and lapidary shops. Open daily. Call for extended summer hours. Fee. (602) 774-8350.

From Meteor Crater, continue to Winslow on I-40. The town is named for F. Edward Winslow who was president of the St. Louis and San Francisco Railroad, and like its neighbor, Holbrook, is devoted to transportation. Situated 30 miles west of the Mogollon Rim, this community serves as a conduit for more remote and scenic areas of the state. Unless you need to stop here, continue east on I-40 for 33 miles to Holbrook.

Known as "The Hub City," because of the transportation lines that intersect here, Holbrook also serves as the seat of Navajo County. It caters to tourists who are on their way to the Painted Desert and Petrified Forest National Park. It's a good place to stretch your legs, pick up a snack, or fill up the car with gas before going on.

THE PAINTED DESERT

From Holbrook continue on I-40 approximately 19 miles to Exit 311. As you approach the parks, the Painted Desert is the area due north of the highway; the Petrified Forest National Park lies south of it. Although the parks are referred to as separate entities, in fact they are contiguous. The Painted Desert offers a superb backdrop for travelers who enjoy the desert at its most delicately pastel, but the Petrified Forest is the better attraction.

Try to time your arrival during the early morning or late afternoon hours. At sun-up or just before sunset, the fallen logs in the Petrified Forest seem most lifelike and the colors of the Painted Desert appear most vibrant.

WHERE TO GO

Painted Desert Inn Museum. One mile north of I-40 at the entrance to the park. This is your first stop. Inside you will learn how both the Painted Desert and the Petrified Forest were formed. Exhibits illustrate the evolution of the Painted Desert, and a short film describes how natural forces turned the forest to stone.

Wander around the displays and pick up information for a self-guided tour of both parks. Open daily. Check for summer and winter hours. Fee. (602) 524-6228.

PETRIFIED FOREST NATIONAL PARK

The Petrified Forest National Park is the greatest and most colorful concentration of petrified wood ever discovered on earth. The park, which consists of 93,431 acres of brilliantly colored stone logs, preserves the glassy remains of an ancient coniferous forest. About 200 million years ago, the trees grew in the highlands to the west and southwest. The area of the present forest was swamp land and as streams carried the dead logs down to this flat, depressed area, they were buried in sediments rich with volcanic ash.

Over eons the chemical process worked its magic. The logs were slowly impregnated with silica until they turned to solid stone. Iron oxide and other minerals then stained the silica producing the stone rainbows we see today. In the process, the logs became stony jewel boxes for quartz and other gemstones that developed in the wood during petrification.

Today each chip and rock is carefully protected. No one is allowed to pick up even the tiniest souvenier. But in ancient times, the people who lived here carved on the petrified wood, chiseled messages on the rocks, and fashioned tools and weapons from the rainbow forest.

You'll want to take a slow drive through the area. If you've stopped at the Painted Desert Visitor Center, you've picked up a pamphlet describing a self-guided drive. This brochure explains all the places you'll want to see. If you don't have a brochure, don't worry because you'll find, as you approach each site, a written description clearly posted. Be sure to stop and get out of your car to see these unusual rock formations. You should hike to **Agate Bridge** in the First Forest. Here a petrified tree fell across a canyon, forming a stoney bridge for eternity. Plan to climb down the 120 steps to **Newspaper Rock,** a large boulder covered with ancient writing. No doubt this served as a kind of local bulletin board, announcing activities and goings-on to the Indians who lived in the area. If you follow all the side roads that are marked in this stoney forest, you'll drive about 38 miles before you reach the south entrance which is your exit point.

WHAT TO DO

Rainbow Forest Museum. Near the south entrance. This is your final stop before leaving the Petrified Forest. Inside you'll see geological exhibits. If you didn't stop at the north entrance, you can learn how the forests were formed here. Open daily. Check for summer and winter hours. Free. (602) 524-6228.

Return to Flagstaff by following US-180 northwest to Holbrook where you'll pick up I-40 west to Flagstaff.

Day Trip 1

MORMON LAKE
HAPPY JACK
WORTH MORE TIME:
PAYSON

MORMON LAKE

Approximately 30 miles southeast of Flagstaff on Mormon Lake Road, Mormon Lake is an optimum destination for a quick, easy, scenic loop through some of Flagstaff's best outdoor country.

To get there from Flagstaff, follow I-17 south to the Lake Mary Road exit. Stay on Lake Mary Road until you reach the Mormon Lake area. As you drive, the road will wind through the Coconino National Forest and will take you near some great fishing lakes. Lake Mary is one of the favorites.

This area is long on scenery but short on facilities. Numerous campgrounds dot the countryside, but wise travelers will carry picnic hampers filled with lunch goodies. You won't find any fast food here, unless, of course, you are especially quick with hook and bait. What you will find, however, is serenity — ponderosa pines trimming lush meadows, backed up by a panorama of the San Francisco Peaks.

As you continue southeast, you'll see a dirt road off to your left (east) which leads to Ashurst Lake. Unless you have a four-wheel drive, avoid this. Dirt roads in this area can be hazardous to the health of your car. Unless you are driving a four-wheel vehicle or a truck, it's advisable to stay on paved surfaces. During the rainy season you can get flooded out, and during the dry periods, these roads can be extremely rough.

Continuing on Lake Mary Road, you'll come to Mormon Lake Road, a dirt byway leading off to your right (west). Take this unpaved road which will loop around Mormon Lake, the largest natural lake in Arizona. Cattle that roamed the meadowland stamped down the earth forming a natural dish that held the winter snowmelt. The Mormons, who remained in this vicinity for many years, ran a dairy and even built a cheese press here. It's not known why they left the area, but probably a drought forced them out.

Over the years the snowmelt continually refilled the depressed area and formed a large natural lake surrounded by open range where cattle graze. The lake is also a haven for ducks and duck hunters.

Adjacent to the water is the village of Mormon Lake, which consists of Montezuma and Mormon Lake lodges, a post office, a dance hall that seats 350 people, a steak house and a general store. During big holiday weekends (including Fourth of July and Labor Day), the dance hall resounds with live entertainment.

WHAT TO DO

Cross-Country Skiing. During the winter you'll find some of the best cross-country skiing in the state. You can drive up and ski for the day or make overnight arrangements at either of two lodges in the area. (See WHERE TO STAY.)

Bicycle Tours. Bicycle enthusiasts rave about touring the Mormon Lake area. Bring your own bicycle or arrange to join a group ride. If you go the entire distance, you'll ride 26 miles around the shoreline. To find out about bicycle tours offered in the Mormon Lake area, call the Arizona Bicycle Club in Phoenix, (602) 264-5478.

WHERE TO EAT

Mormon Lake Lodge. Mormon Lake. The menu features seven kinds of steaks, all reasonably priced. During the summer, the lodge is open for breakfast, lunch and dinner. In winter, only dinner is served during the week with all meals available on the weekends. $$; □. (602) 354-2220.

WHERE TO STAY

Montezuma Lodge. Mormon Lake. Follow the Mormon Lake dirt road three miles to the lodge. Guests can stay in 20 well-equipped kitchenette cabins nestled in the woods against the Mormon Mountains. This is a favorite "ride-in" stop for bicyclists who come, packs on their backs, to rest and then ride in the area. In summer, the main lodge is used only for potluck suppers and friendly get-togethers.

During the winter, the road to the lodge is closed. Guests ski in to their cabins, stopping first to check in at the General Store (which during the winter months sells ski equipment instead of supplies). There you can get outfitted and take ski lessons and cross-country ski directly to your cabin door. The lodge runs a shuttle that delivers your gear to the cabins. During these snow bound months, the owner/operator cooks meals for the guests who gather in the main lodge for food and conversation after a brisk day of exploring. $-$$; □. (602) 354-2220.

Mormon Lake Lodge. Mormon Lake. From Lake Mary Road, turn right onto Mormon Lake Road and continue for nine miles to the lodge. (You will pass Montezuma Lodge.) Here are ten sleeping units — four motel rooms and six cabins (cooking facilities are in two of the cabins). $-$$; □. (602) 354-2227.

HAPPY JACK

Another 12 miles southwest on Lake Mary Road you'll come to Happy Jack, a logging community. You'll see campgrounds and some private cabins tucked away on this not-so-beaten path. From Happy Jack you have a few options. You can continue to the junction with A-87 and follow A-87 northeast to Winslow. From Winslow, follow US-180 back to Flagstaff.

Or you may follow lake Mary Road to the junction of A-87 and take A-87 to Strawberry and Pine, and then follow General Crook Highway west to Camp Verde. There you can pick up I-17 north and continue to Flagstaff. Along the way, you can stop at Montezuma Castle and Montezuma Well. (See DAY TRIP 2, NORTH FROM PHOENIX).

WORTH MORE TIME:
PAYSON

A third option is to follow Lake Mary Road south to A-87 and continue on A-87 to Payson. See DAY TRIP 2, NORTHEAST FROM PHOENIX for more details on what to see and do around this community.

Day Trip 1

OAK CREEK/SEDONA
WORTH MORE TIME:
MONTEZUMA WELL AND MONTEZUMA CASTLE

OAK CREEK

From Flagstaff, head due south on A-179 to Oak Creek and Sedona. (Refer to DAY TRIP 3, NORTH OF PHOENIX for all there is to do and see here.) From Flagstaff, the trip to Sedona takes less than an hour.

WORTH MORE TIME:
MONTEZUMA WELL AND
MONTEZUMA CASTLE

From Sedona, stay on A-179 south to its junction with I-17. To visit Montezuma Castle or Montezuma Well, drive south on I-17 to the exits marked for each. (See DAY TRIP 2, NORTH OF PHOENIX for additional information on these historic sites). One fee covers both the castle and the well. (602) 567-3322.

Day Trip 1

JEROME
PRESCOTT

JEROME

Follow US-89A due south from Flagstaff. You'll drive about an hour to reach Jerome, a charming semi-ghost town. (Read about Jerome in DAY TRIP 2, NORTH OF PHOENIX.)

PRESCOTT

From Jerome, continue 41 miles southwest on US-89A to Prescott, Arizona's picturesque community famous for its Victorian homes and historical significance. Here territorial Arizona springs to life. The first capital of the Arizona Territory, Prescott ultimately lost its bid to become the permanent state capital to Phoenix. Still much Arizona history was made here and, fortunately for visitors, remains well-preserved. For more information, see DAY TRIP 1, NORTH FROM PHOENIX.

Day Trip 1

WILLIAMS
GRAND CANYON CAVERNS

WILLIAMS

From Flagstaff, drive west 32 miles on I-40 across the golden meadowland known as Garland Prairie. During spring and summer, the meadow is a carpet of wildflowers. The fields shimmer with azure blues and dashing reds. As you continue toward Williams you drive through the pine-scented, lush greenery of the **Kaibab National Forest.**

Called "The Gateway to the Grand Canyon," Williams is named for William S. (or Old Bill) Williams, a master trapper and Indian Scout who traveled the Santa Fe Trail during the 1820s. A rugged six-foot, one-inch eccentric, he was known to drink and gamble excessively. Called the "lone wolf" of trappers, like many of the mountain men of his day, Old Bill spent most of his time working and sleeping in the wilderness. He only emerged from the mountains long enough to lose his money fast. Then he'd retreat to the wilds to trap and restock his supply of furs. Soon he'd reappear in town, get cash, and start the cycle again.

Although mountain men like Old Bill Williams are remembered primarily as trappers, they played a key role in Arizona history. True, they were an environmental disaster, wiping out the entire populations of grizzlies and beavers which once roamed the forests and swam in the streams. But as explorers, mappers and later guides for the military, these reclusive individuals provided invaluable services. Their knowledge of the wilderness made it possible to open the land for the settlers who followed.

Today the spirit of Old Bill Williams is kept alive through the Bill Williams Mountain Men who have their headquarters in Williams. If you are in town during any of the town's celebrations (see the Festival section), you may have an opportunity to see them in full regalia, dressed in furs and leather. This group of Williams men meets regularly to celebrate the spirit of Old Bill and reenact the mountain men's unique period of frontier history. They ride in parades, take part in rodeos and whoop it up in festivities in Williams and elsewhere throughout the state.

Like many northern Arizona communities, Williams is a sportsman's paradise. The town sits in the shadow of Bill Williams Mountain, a 9286-foot high peak just south of this small community. Good walking trails scale both sides of the mountain. Seven fishing lakes, many with cabins and boating facilities, surround the town. During the winter, there's a small (450-foot vertical drop) downhill ski run. In addition to skiing, **The Benham Snow Play Area,** just south of town on County Road 173, echoes with "snow tubers," kids and adults careening down snowy slopes in inner tubes. For complete information on camping, fishing and hiking in the vicinity, visit or write the Williams Grand Canyon Chamber of Commerce, 820 W. Bill Williams Ave., Williams, AZ 86046 or call (602) 635-2041.

WHERE TO GO

Grand Canyon Deer Farm. 100 Deer Farm Road. As you drive toward Williams from Flagstaff, you'll see this unusual petting zoo facing I-40 eight miles east of Williams, some 24 miles west of Flagstaff. This is a fun stop for families with children. Adults who enjoy observing eight varieties of these graceful animals will also like this farm. Some deer are common to Arizona and other areas of the U.S. but there are more unusual types such as Japanese Sika deer and a herd of Spotted Fallow, a type found in the Mediterranean. Open every day during the summer, this small, privately-owned facility is closed from Thanksgiving Day through March. Phone for specific hours. Fee. (602) 635-2357.

The Little Grand Canyon (also called Sycamore Point). Twelve miles south of White Horse Lake on forest service road 110. This is a side trip for adventurous explorers. Locals call this "The Little Grand Canyon" and when you see it, you'll understand why. Follow the paved County Road, #173, south of Williams (toward Perkinsville and Jerome) to the unpaved forest service road 110, which leads to White Horse Lake. Drive 12 miles south on Forest Service Road 119, a rugged, bumpy road to Sycamore Point. When you arrive, feast your eyes on the steep limestone walls and pillars of sandstone which form this canyon.

Although Oak Creek Canyon offers a more dramatic vertical drop, and the Sedona area has more rocky sculptures, the Little Grand Canyon exudes a solitary beauty. With its rocky spires and stands of aspen, oak and sycamore, it is largely undiscovered and appeals to those invididuals who like the thrill of discovering a magestic, pristine jewel. Rugged adventurers can hike among the cliffs and rock formations. Since there are no established trails or facilities here, inexperienced hikers should not attempt to walk in this wilderness.

GRAND CANYON CAVERNS

Continue west approximately 44 miles on I-40 through Ash Fork, which calls itself the flagstone capitol of the world, and go on to Seligman. Exit the interstate and pick up A-66, or "Old 66." Follow A-66 about 25 miles to the Grand Canyon Caverns.

Here is one of the world's largest completely dry cave systems. Meandering 21 stories beneath the earth, the well-preserved Grand Canyon Caverns are known to be closely related geologically to the Grand Canyon. Yet because of its off-the-beaten path location, tourists often ignore it. Professional cave explorers are well acquainted with the caverns and excavation goes on continually because experts are certain that more rocky rooms wait to be discovered.

You'll enter through a commercial center which has a coffee shop, motel, gift shop and airstrip for private planes. A 45-minute guided tour leads you through the expanse of vaulted rooms filled with colorful rock formations. You'll wander through mysterious passageways and hear an intriguing commentary about the history of the caves. But for all its wild beauty, this is a comfortable experience for explorers of all ages. The paths are paved and the formations well lit.

The caverns became general knowledge in 1927 when a heavy rain widened the natural funnel-shaped opening to the upper level. However, the Hualapai (Wal'-pee) Indians, a tribe that lived here centuries ago, were familiar with that level of the caverns. Even today, elders caution young people that the original entrance is a sacred place and should be observed as such.

From fossils imbedded in the redwall limestone, scientists have determined that many prehistoric sea and land dwellers once lived in these caves. Fossils of a giant ground sloth, estimated to have lived here over 20,000 years ago, were also discovered in the caverns. Open daily. Closed Christmas eve and day and for the last three weeks of January. Fee. (602) 422-3223.

To return to Flagstaff, follow old A-66 east to Seligman. Pick up I-40 east through Williams to Flagstaff.

Day Trip 1

THE SOUTH RIM OF
THE GRAND CANYON

THE SOUTH RIM OF
THE GRAND CANYON

From Flagstaff, drive north on US-180 approximately 60 miles to Grand Canyon Village, headquarters for this most spectacular national park. All visitors to Arizona put the Grand Canyon at the top of their "must see" list, but few realize that the Grand Canyon is actually two parks: the North Rim and the South Rim. The South park is closer to Phoenix. It is located 223 miles north of that city, and is open to tourists all year. The more rugged and remote North Rim is a 230-mile drive from the southern park. Although it is possible to "do" the South Rim of the Grand Canyon in a long day's trip starting and ending in Phoenix, the experience is exhausting. It is far better to use Flagstaff as your headquarters if you plan to see the canyon in one day. Better yet, stay overnight in the Grand Canyon park area.

Should you decide to see both rims, you'll be in for two distinctly different experiences. The North Rim, more than 1000 feet higher than the South Rim, is the more remote and rugged park. It is closed from late fall to mid-spring because the roads are snowed in from about late October to mid-May. Facilities at the North Rim exist on a smaller, more rustic scale. In contrast, although the facilities at the South Rim are superb, it's often crowded during the summer.

The fascination with the Grand Canyon spans every age, nationality and experience. The view into the chasm appears pure illusion, for it seems that nothing can be that deep, that mysterious, that endless.

While volumes have been written about its majesty, no words or pictures can contain the happy shock of coming upon it. One writer notes that people who stare across and into the magnificent abyss, no matter how many pictures they've seen of it, find themselves instinctively looking back to check that the earth they're standing on is solid.

Although you may suppose that it will be enough for you to just stand and gaze at this massive split in the heart of the earth, once you arrive you'll discover that you may want to participate more fully in the canyon experience. Then you must decide how to do it, for there are many ways to see the South Rim. You can travel on foot, on horseback, or cling to a mule. You can view the Grand Canyon from the top down: flying over it in a small plane or helicopter; or from the bottom up: riding the torrents of the Colorado River rapids. For more information on the South Rim, call the National Park Service (602) 638-7888. During the busy tourist season (spring, summer and early fall), you'll need reservations for either camping or lodging facilities. You must also make prior arrangements if you plan to journey into the canyon for an overnight hike or pack trip because overnight hikers and campers must have permits. As with all national parks, there is an entrance fee.

WHERE TO GO

Grand Canyon IMAX Theatre. Seven miles south of the South Rim on A-64/US-180 in Tusayan (too'-see-an). If you haven't experienced an IMAX film, you're in for a treat. An IMAX film puts you into the action. You sit surrounded by a six-track stereophonic soundtrack, looking up at a 70-foot-high screen. Even if you've seen any of the other IMAX films (they cover many subjects from time to outer space), see this one. "The Grand Canyon — The Hidden Secrets" is the most popular of IMAX productions shown in this country. In 34 minutes you get a crash course on the Grand Canyon and the Colorado River and their geography, geology, history and anthropology.

Thanks to the wonders of photographic magic, you even experience a wild river ride down the rapids of the Colorado River. The film is shown daily. For schedule information, telephone or write to The Grand Canyon IMAX Theatre, P. O. Box 1397, Grand Canyon, AZ 86023-1397. Fee. (602) 638-2203.

Visitors Center. In the Grand Canyon National Park, one mile east of Grand Canyon Village on Village Loop Drive. This should be your first stop once you enter the park. No matter how you choose to experience the canyon, you'll get more out of it if you have an understanding of how grand it really is.

Spend some time studying the exhibits and dioramas describing the formation of the canyon and the flora and fauna in the area. You'll find brochures and information on several self-guided walking tours which traverse the rim. Here you can also pick up trail maps for hiking into the canyon and get information on driving tours along the East Rim and West Rim drives.

East Rim Drive. A paved road leads from the visitors center past the **Yavapai Museum,** a delightful and informative geological facility, to Mather, Yaki and Grand View points. The road continues to Desert View, a spectacular lookout 25 miles east of Grand Canyon Village. Along the way, you may stop at any of the turn outs to experience the panorama of the Canyon. This is an especially impressive drive in the early morning hours or just before sunset when the colors of the canyon are their richest.

West Rim Drive. This takes you past Powell Memorial and Hopi, Mohave and Pima points — equally outstanding places from which to observe the majesty of the canyon. This drive ends at Hermit's Rest. From April through September, the West Rim road is limited to tour buses to relieve traffic congestion and help preserve the ecological integrity of the canyon. For information about the bus tours, inquire at the visitors center.

Don't leave the visitors center without browsing through the selection of scientific and illustrated books for sale. The more you can learn about the canyon, the more you'll enjoy your visit. Even non scientific types should know that this region encompasses five of the Northern Hemisphere's seven ecological zones, and that no other place in the world so clearly illustrates such a vast panorama of time. Open daily. Free. (602) 638-7888.

El Tovar Hotel. On Village Loop Drive, Fred Harvey, Inc., P. O. Box 699, Grand Canyon, AZ 86023. From the visitors center follow Village Loop Drive west about a half mile to the first right turn. This road takes you to the parking lot for El Tovar. Even if you do not intend to stay or eat at this hotel, (see WHERE TO EAT AND WHERE TO STAY sections) make it a point to visit this historic place. El Tovar is a rambling, wooden hotel which has long served as headquarters for activity at the South Rim. On any day, as you stand in the spacious, high-ceilinged lobby, you may hear a dozen different languages, see sunburned hikers who have just emerged from the canyon floor, listen to river rafters still riding high on their exhilaration, and see celebrities and dignitaries who have come to relax in the stately splendor afforded by this charming setting. (602) 638-2631.

Bright Angel Trail. As you leave El Tovar, turn left and follow the Rim Walk toward Bright Angel Lodge. There's a sign pointing to the Bright Angel trail, a well-maintained hiking path which twists and turns 20.6 miles into the canyon floor.

For the first half-mile, Bright Angel is gentle enough for even non hikers to negotiate without any special equipment other than good walking shoes. However, as you peer down the trail from the Rim, you'll see a splash of deep green in the distance. The green glistens against the sunbleached yellows, oranges and peach tones of the Grand Canyon. This is **Indian Gardens,** a 4.4-mile hike from the top. The trek to Indian Gardens takes you through man-made tunnels and down a series of steep switchbacks. You can rest and picnic at this remarkable natural oasis which is shaded by tall cottonwood trees. The hike to Indian Gardens is an excellent round-trip day experience which gives you a good workout and a sense of the serenity of the inner Canyon.

The less ambitious may prefer a 15-minute walk down Bright Angel trail. Go at least as far as the first tunnel or hole-in-the-rock. Remember, it will take you twice as long, or a half-hour, to walk back up. Even this short excursion will give you a feeling for the grandeur of the canyon, an understanding which you can never get from standing at the Rim and looking down into it.

WHERE TO EAT

El Tovar. In the park on Village Loop Drive. Count on hearty breakfasts and superb views from the dining room window. Pancakes are light and fluffy, and the syrup hot. Lunches and dinners are more elegant. The food and the service rival those of any fine restaurant in the Phoenix or Tucson area. During the spring, summer and early fall, reservations are recommended for dinner. $$; □. (602) 638-2631.

WHERE TO STAY

El Tovar. In the park on Village Loop Drive, Fred Harvey, Inc., P. O. Box 699, Grand Canyon, AZ 86023. Because this is an historic hotel, each room is different — some large and airy; others smaller — but the accommodations are uniformly charming. If you are looking for atmosphere and convenience, El Tovar is an outstanding choice. $$; □. (602) 638-2631.

Grand Canyon Squire Inn. One mile south of the entrance to Grand Canyon National Park and one-half mile north of Grand Canyon National Park Airport on US-180/AZ-64. The Grand Canyon Squire Inn is a newer resort and conference center with meeting rooms, continental cuisine and tennis courts. For information, write to Grand Canyon Squire Inn, P. O. Box 130, Grand Canyon, AZ 86023-0130. $$; □. (602) 638-2681.

For a complete listing of all motel accommodations and camping facilities available in the park, contact the Superintendent, Grand Canyon National Park, Grand Canyon, AZ 86023, or call (602) 638-7888.

WHAT ELSE TO DO

Hiking and Backpacking. For information on hiking and trail services in the park, contact Grand Canyon Hiker Services or the National Park Service Concessionaire for hiking and backpacking. A network of trails of varying difficulty criss-cross the canyon. Some lead to remote destinations; others are more accessible. Hikers of any skill and interest can have a rewarding experience. From April to November, inquire about hiking and backpacking by writing to Grand Canyon Hiker Services, P. O. Box 735, Grand Canyon, AZ 86023, (602) 638-2391. At any time during the year, you can write to Grand Canyon Hiker Services at P. O. Box 2997, East Flagstaff, AZ 86003, or call (602) 526-0924.

Muleback Trips. Mules descend the Bright Angel Trail at the South Rim on full-day, half-day, and overnight trips. This is a strenuous trip. Good physical condition is a *must*. Reservations are mandatory from May through October. Fee. For information about these excursions, contact Grand Canyon National Park Lodges, Reservations Department, P. O. Box 699, Grand Canyon, AZ 86023, or call (602) 638-2401.

Colorado River Trips. Motor-powered raft and rowing trips are regularly scheduled down the Colorado River during the summer months. Various kinds of boats and trips are geared to different types of travelers. You can choose anything from a rugged few weeks of boating and hiking to an exciting but still relaxing experience.

If you plan only one "outdoorsy" experience in your lifetime, this should be it. Nothing beats it. The Colorado River not only has the most rapids, but the most exciting rapids of any river, and there is only one Grand Canyon in the entire world to provide such a glorious backdrop for the thrills. If you're worried about roughing it, don't be. There are plenty of luxuries, including excellent food and even cakes baked fresh on the beach. For thrills in an incomparable setting, this trip cannot be equaled.

Would-be river rats (the local terminology for those who've run the river) should be in good physical condition. Each rafting company has its own list of requirements. Fee. For a complete listing of companies, write or telephone the National Park Service at the Grand Canyon. Address inquiries to the Superintendent, Grand Canyon National Park, Grand Canyon, AZ 86023, or call (602) 638-7888.

Festivals
and
Celebrations

JANUARY

Phoenix Area

Fiesta Bowl Day, Tempe. This is becoming one of the major college bowls in the country and each year attracts top university football talent. (602) 952-1280.

Lost Dutchman Days, Apache Junction. The Lost Dutchman lives again each year during the three-day rodeo, parade, arts and craft exhibit, antique car show and carnival. (602) 982-3141.

Tucson Area

American Hot Rod Association's Winter Nationals, Tucson. The biggest national drag race goes on for four days at Tucson Dragway. (602) 885-1291.

FEBRUARY

Phoenix Area

Parada del Sol, Scottsdale. Enjoy top professional rodeo, an elaborate horse-drawn parade and wild western fun. Scottsdale celebrates the entire week as the town dresses, thinks and acts Western. (602) 994-1447.

Yuma Crossing Day, Yuma. This festival celebrates the "Crossing of the Fathers" when the Spanish crossed the Colorado River into Arizona to settle the territory. Dance performances and exhibits are held at cultural and historical facilities throughout the area. Horse-drawn wagons shuttle visitors to and from each facility. (602) 783-8020.

Quartzsite Annual Gem and Mineral Show, Quartzsite. Thousands of rockhounds flock each year to this tiny desert community to buy and sell at one of the world's largest gem and mineral shows. See demonstrations of rock tumbling and learn about the world of gems. (602) 927-6325.

Tucson Area

Tubac Arts Festival, Tubac. A nine-day outdoor festival featuring international craftspeople. Demonstrations, exhibits and food booths make this a perennial favorite. (602) 398-2704.

MARCH

Phoenix Area

Phoenix Rodeo of Rodeos, Phoenix. Professional cowboys converge on Phoenix to compete in a national indoor rodeo of top calibre. An impressive parade in downtown Phoenix highlights the week's festivities. (602) 264-0808.

Old Town Tempe Spring Festival of the Arts, Tempe. The center of Tempe becomes a shopper's paradise as artists and craftsmen from all over the country set up booths to show and sell their wares. You'll find everything from junque to true art — often at bargain prices. (602) 967-4877.

Tucson Area

La Fiesta de Los Vaqueros, Tucson. This is Tucson's *big* rodeo. Usually held in February, it is kicked off by the longest nonmechanized parade in the world. (602) 792-1212.

Tombstone Territorial Days, Tombstone. This tiny town celebrates its beginnings with a carnival of fun. Shoot-outs, the Arizona Firehose Cart Championship and a pet parade make this fun. (602) 457-2211.

APRIL

Phoenix Area

Arid Land Plant Show, Superior. Held at the Boyce Thompson Southwestern Arboretum, this show features a wide variety of drought-resistant trees, shrubs, cacti and succulents from as far away as

Australia and Africa. Gardeners find this a great place to look, browse and buy. Learn how nature equips these beautiful, unusual plants to survive in water-short lands. (602) 689-2811.

Heard Museum Indian Fair, Phoenix. Stroll the museum grounds and see dances, arts, crafts and exhibits from many Arizona Indian tribes. Munch on delicious Navajo fry bread, made hot on the grounds, and other native delicacies. Bring the entire family for this popular, authentic Native American fair. (602) 252-8848.

Tucson Area

San Xavier (Ha-veer') Pageant and Fiesta, San Xavier Mission. This dramatic event is held the Friday after Easter and begins in late afternoon with over 100 Indian dancers celebrating the history of the mission. As night falls, 100 bonfires are lit and the coming of Father Garces, who built the present mission, and Father Kino, who opened the land for the Spanish, is commemorated through narration and drama. More than 20 costumed horsemen ride into the area lit by bonfires, and the evening ends with a spectacular procession of worshippers, the joyous pealing of bells and fireworks. Throughout the weekend, the Papago Indians host a food and crafts market. (602) 622-6911.

Fiesta de la Placita, Tucson. The Hispanic community of Tucson turns out for a bilingual, full-fledged Mexican fiesta full of slowly-simmered Mexican food, pinata games, dancing and music. Everyone, regardless of heritage, is invited to attend. (602) 622-6911.

Pioneer Days, Tucson. This two-day festival celebrates the history of Tucson during the nineteenth century and features dancing of all kinds — from Indian to barn dances. There are Western food booths, mountain men, and brightly costumed camp ladies and military men. A spectacular Military Field Day includes reenactments of frontier battles. Be sure to sample the "Old West BBQ." Pioneer crafts are displayed and sold. (602) 622-6911.

La Vuelta de Bisbee, Bisbee. A three-day bicycle race attracts riders from all over the country who compete on the tortuously steep course through this mining town. (602) 432-2141.

MAY

Phoenix Area

George Phippen Memorial Invitational Western Art Show and Sale, Prescott. This show, held over Memorial Day Weekend, attracts Western artists from all over the country. Well-known names compete for medals, and unknowns have a chance to be discovered. There's an art auction, and reception so that the public can meet the show's painters and sculptors. (602) 445-2000.

Flagstaff Area

Bill Williams Rendezvous Days, Williams. This festival is held on Memorial Day weekend. In addition to the in-town arts and crafts booths, cow-chip throwing contests, live music and food booths, the Williams city park hosts an authentic Mountain Men Rendezvous. Here men and women from around the country camp (1840s style) in teepees and compete in authentic Mountain Man black powder events. The "Raw Egg Shoot" is a favorite. If a contestant misses the egg, he eats it. See Mountain Men compete in the "Seneca Run," which combines all wilderness skills into one marathon event. Men must shoot, throw a tomahawk, canoe, run, set a bear trap and light a fire. (602) 635-2041.

JUNE

Phoenix Area

Old Time Country Music Festival, Payson. All kinds of bands including bluegrass, country and buck-dancing, compete in this nationally recognized music festival. (602) 474-4515.

Annual Chili Cookoff, Payson. If you think a chili cookoff is full of beans, think again. This is a world-class cooking event — complete with a parade. Sample all the chefs' best recipes. (602) 474-4515.

Annual Square Dance Festival, Prescott. Pick up some new twists and dips and watch teams from around the country compete in this most American dance experience. This is a fun festival for dancers and toe-tappers. (602) 445-4539.

International Innertube Race, Parker. Hundreds of people, dressed in outlandish costumes, converge on the Colorado River to compete in a seven-mile race. (602) 669-2174.

Tucson Area

Bisbee Renaissance Festival, Bisbee. A celebration of Bisbee's rebirth. Watch the jousting and enjoy the food, arts and crafts and merrymaking. (602) 432-2141.

JULY

Phoenix Area

Prescott Frontier Days and Rodeo, Prescott. The town turns out for the Fourth of July weekend in flag-waving frontier style with a glittering parade, rugged professional rodeo (the oldest rodeo in the country), dancing and general wild fun. In Arizona, Prescott's Whiskey Row is *the* place to be this weekend. (602) 445-2000.

Championship Loggers/Sawdust Festival, Payson. This is one of the biggest sawdust festivals in the country where loggers come to show off their skills in competition. Among the events scheduled are rolling pin throws (a ladies' contest), crosscut sawing, precision cutting, and axe throwing. Loggers from all over the country converge here for this festival. (602) 474-4515.

AUGUST

Flagstaff Area

Arizona Cowpunchers' Reunion and Old Timers' Rodeo, Williams. If you want to see real, working cowboys, this is the place to come. Only working cowboys are allowed to compete. All events involve skills these cowboys use in their profession. Spectators can watch three-man teams compete in a wild horse race where men must catch, saddle and ride a wild horse across a finish line. Another favorite is the wild cow milking contest where two-man teams rope and milk a cow, catching the milk in a coke bottle. This is not as crazy as it sounds, because often a wild cow won't nurse her baby. Cowboys must catch and milk the cow, then put the milk into a coke bottle, so they can save the young calf. (602) 635-2041.

Phoenix Area

Payson Annual Continuous Rodeo, Payson. See the world's oldest continuously-held professional rodeo. Watch cowboys from around the world ride bucking broncos and rope steers while they compete for big money. The rodeo weekend includes all kinds of Western festivities. (602) 474-4515.

SEPTEMBER

Phoenix Area

Annual State Championship Old Time Fiddlers Contest, Payson. This is one of Payson's most famous festivals. You can hear fiddlers from all over the state compete with their fanciest fingerwork. This is a delightful art form for spectators as well as contestants. (602) 474-4958.

National Indian Day, Parker. This is celebrated in Manataba Park the last Friday of September and the following Saturday. The four tribes in the area, plus others from throughout the Southwest converge for traditional games, singing, dances and other activities. Arts and crafts and traditional foods are sold. The celebration begins in mid-afternoon and picks up toward evening. (602) 669-2174.

Flagstaff Area

Annual Navajo Nation Fair, Window Rock. Window Rock is the headquarters for the Navajo Nation. Feast your eyes on fine Navajo arts and crafts and your tummies on hot Navajo fry bread dripping with honey. There's even a Navajo Fry Bread-making contest, as well as horse racing, rodeos, a parade and an authentic Indian pow-wow. Other events include a 10,000-meter run and traditional Navajo singing and dancing competition. (602) 871-4417.

OCTOBER

Phoenix Area

Arizona State Fair, Phoenix. Livestock shows, exhibits, big name entertainment and a carnival are just part of the action when the annual State Fair comes to town. (602) 252-6771.

Tucson Area

Helldorado Days, Tombstone. This is the event which puts Tombstone on the map every year. If you ever wondered what the Old West was like, come to Helldorado Days and find out. Shoot-outs, a fast-draw contest and a parade add to the general wild Western craziness. (602) 457-2211.

NOVEMBER

Phoenix Area

Fountain Festival of the Arts, Fountain Hills. More than 200 artists, artisans and craftspeople move into Fountain Hills for a three-day show and sale. The juried competition attracts some of the finest artists in the country. The pottery and sculptures are always outstanding. (602) 837-1654.

Annual Swiss Village Christmas Lighting, Payson. Set among Payson's pine forests, the Swiss village looks amazingly appropriate when dressed for Christmas. The celebration brings out the entire town. (602) 474-4515.

DECEMBER

Nearly every community has a Christmas tradition. Festivals abound. For a more complete listing, consult the Chambers of Commerce in each city. Below is a sampling of what happens during the holiday season.

Phoenix Area

Old Town Tempe Fall Festival of the Arts, Tempe. If you miss the Spring Festival, come to this one. Mill Avenue, the main street of town, becomes a bazaar of arts, crafts and unusual collectibles as artists set up booths to show their wares. The art on display is often terrific and always interesting. (602) 967-4877.

Victorian Christmas at Heritage Square, Phoenix. Phoenix turns back the clock to the 1800s as Dickens comes to the desert. The dress at this celebration is heavy with velvet and lace. Christmas stories are read aloud, choirs sing, and the historical district glows with the spirit of Christmases past. (602) 262-5071.

Christmas Parade and Courthouse Lighting, Prescott. With its Victorian setting in place all year long, Christmas comes naturally to Prescott. The entire town turns out for the parade and comes to the square to see the courthouse blaze with colorful lights. (602) 445-2000.

Tucson Area

Luminaria Night, Tucson. The Tucson Botanical Garden is lit by hundreds of luminarias (lighted votive candles nestled into brown paper bags which are filled part way with sand). Mariachis, bands, Yaqui Indian dancers and other musicians add to the festivities. (602) 624-1817.

Tumacacori Fiesta, Tumacacori. Folk dancing, music, food and crafts from many of Santa Cruz County's cultural groups make this a special Southwestern holiday celebration. (602) 398-2341.

Worth More Time

Christmas Boat Parade of Lights, Lake Havasu. Watch as gaily trimmed and lighted houseboats glide across Lake Havasu in an unusual salute to the season. (602) 855-2178.

Holiday boat parades also are held on Lake Mead and Lake Mohave. Check with the local Chambers of Commerce at Bullhead City, (602) 754-4121, and Parker, (602) 669-2174, for dates and times.

THE GREAT OUTDOORS

National Parks

Arizona is studded with a wonderland of national parks, monuments and forests. Although the state is vast in its physical size, popular parks can fill up quickly. It's always wise to write or call ahead for information, instructions, camping permits, and other details when planning a visit to a national recreation site.

Grand Canyon National Park
Back Country Reservation Office
P. O. Box 129
Grand Canyon, AZ 86023
(602) 638-2474

Canyon de Chelly (Shay) National Monument
Box 588
Chinle, AZ 86503
(602) 674-5436

Prescott National Forest
2323 E. Greenlaw Lane
Flagstaff, AZ 86001
(602) 527-7400

Kaibab National Forest
Sixth Street
Williams, AZ 86046
(602) 635-2181

Apache-Sitgreaves National Forest
P. O. Box 649
Springerville, AZ 85938
(602) 333-4301

In addition to forests, monuments and parks operated by the federal government, other public land in Arizona is under the direction of the U. S. Bureau of Land Management (BLM). Information about hiking or camping on BLM lands is available from the following address:

Bureau of Land Management
Arizona State Office
Siete Square
3707 North Seventh St.
Phoenix, AZ 85014
(602) 241-5501

Indian Reservations

Arizona is home to 14 Indian tribes representing nearly 160,000 people. A total of 20 reservations cover more than 19 million acres. As you read this list, you will see many hyphenated tribal names. Over the years, the U. S. government has combined tribes, giving them new homes together on a single reservation. Nevertheless, each has managed to retain its own distinct heritage.

Visitors who wish to travel on Indian reservations may do so without prior permission. However, if you want to know where to go to buy arts or crafts or observe dances, celebrations or rodeos, you should call ahead or write to the tribal office for dates, times and locations. Following is a brief description and location of each tribe.

Ak-Chin Reservation, 56 miles south of Phoenix in Pinal County. This tribe is noted for basketry.
Ak-Chin Indian Community
Rt. 2, Box 27
Maricopa, AZ 85239
(602) 568-2227

Camp Verde Reservation, 94 miles north of Phoenix in Yavapai County. This reservation includes Montezuma Castle National Monument and Montezuma Well. Basketry is the major art form.
Yavapai-Apache Indian Community
P. O. Box 1188
Camp Verde, AZ 86322
(602) 567-3649

Cocopah East and West Reservations, 12 miles southwest of Yuma in Yuma County. This tribe is well known for its intricate beadwork.
Cocopah Tribal Council
Bin "G"
Somerton, AZ 85350
(602) 627-2102

Colorado River Reservation, 189 miles west of Phoenix in Yuma County. Collectors may want to buy baskets, beadwork and Indian motif wall clocks made by these tribes.
Colorado River Indian Tribes
Rt. 1, Box 23-B
Parker, AZ 85344
(602) 669-9211

Fort Apache Reservation, 194 miles northeast of Phoenix in Apache, Gila and Navajo counties. The Apache Tribe owns and operates Apache Sunrise Resort, a ski lodge and resort facility. Skiing aside, the people create excellent beadwork and the highly-prized "Burden Baskets," wonderfully woven baskets which are trimmed with leather thongs and silver metal "bells."
White Mountain Apache Tribe
P. O. Box 700
Whiteriver, AZ 85941
(602) 338-4346

Fort McDowell Reservation, 36 miles northeast of Phoenix in Maricopa County. The Fort McDowell Indians manufacture jojoba bean oil, which is a superb substitute for the environmentally scarce whale oil. Basketry is a specialty.
Mohave-Apache Tribal Council
P. O. Box 17779
Fountain Hills, AZ 85268
(602) 990-0995

Fort Mojave Reservation, 236 miles northwest of Phoenix in Mohave County. This reservation borders Arizona, Nevada and California; tribal headquarters are located in California. The Fort Mojave Indians are noted for their beadwork.
Fort Mojave Tribal Council
P. O. Box 888
500 Merriman Ave.
Needles, CA 92363
(619) 326-4591

Fort Yuma Reservation, 185 miles southwest of Phoenix in Yuma County, this reservation borders Arizona and California. Information may be obtained by writing to an Arizona address or by calling the tribal headquarters in California. Collectors may buy beadwork and other artifacts from this tribe.
Quechan Tribal Council
P. O. Box 1352
Yuma, AZ 85364
(619) 572-0213

Gila (Hee'-la) River Reservation, 40 miles south of Phoenix in Maricopa and Pinal counties. Pima basketry and Maricopa pottery are prized native items produced by the Pimas and Maricopas.
Gila River Indian Community
P. O. Box 97
Sacaton, AZ 85247
(602) 963-4323 or (602) 562-3311

Havasupai (Have-a-sue'-pie) Reservation, at the bottom of the Grand Canyon via an eight-mile trail from Hilltop to Supai. The people of the "Blue-Green Waters" are best known for their exquisite, remote reservation reachable only by mule or foot. The Havasupais produce basketry and beadwork.
Havasupai Tribal Council
P. O. Box 10
Supai, AZ 86435
(602) 448-2961 or (602) 448-2731

Hopi (Hoe'-pee) Reservation, 323 miles northeast of Phoenix in Coconino and Navajo counties. The Hopi produce an assortment of art and collectibles. Basketry and plaques are exquisite, but Hopi are better known for handcarved and painted kachina dolls which are spirits of the gods worshipped by this tribe. The Hopi are also leaders in silver and gold jewelry, crafts and pottery.
Hopi Tribe Council
P. O. Box 123
Kyakotsmovi, AZ 86039
(602) 734-2445

Hualapai (Wall'-pie) Reservation, 252 miles northwest of Phoenix in Coconino, Yavapai and Mohave counties. Dolls and basketry are the primary art forms of this tribe.
Hualapai Tribal Council
P. O. Box 168
Peach Springs, AZ 86434
(602) 769-2216

Kaibab-Paiute (Kigh'-bab - Pie'-ute) Reservation, 398 miles north of Phoenix in Mohave County. This tribe specializes in coiled shallow baskets known as "wedding baskets."
Kaibab-Paiute Tribal Council
Tribal Affairs Building, Pipe Springs Rt.
Fredonia, AZ 86022
(602) 643-7245

Navajo Reservation, 356 miles northeast of Phoenix in Apache, Coconino and Navajo counties. Best known for their museum-quality hand-woven rugs and blankets, the Navajo also create magnificent silver crafts and some basketry.
Cultural Resources Department
Visitor Services
P. O. Box 308
Window Rock, AZ 86515
(602) 871-4941

Papago (Pap'-ago) Reservation, 136 miles south of Phoenix (adjacent to the city of Tucson), this reservation stretches across Maricopa, Pinal and Pima counties. Best known for its distinctive and valuable basketry, the tribe also produces fine pottery.
Papago Tribal Council
P. O. Box 837
Sells, AZ 85634
(602) 383-2221

Pascua-Yaqui Reservation, 135 miles southwest of Phoenix (adjacent to the city of Tucson) in Pima County. Collectors appreciate the "Deer Dance" statues and cultural paintings created by the children of the tribe.
Pascua-Yaqui Tribal Council
4821 W. Calle Vicam
Tucson, AZ 85706
(602) 883-2838

Salt River Reservation, 15 miles northeast of Phoenix adjacent to the city of Scottsdale. The Salt River Indians produce basketry and pottery.
Salt River Pima-Maricopa Tribal Council
Rt. 1, Box 216
Scottsdale, AZ 85256
(602) 941-7277

San Carlos Reservation, 115 miles northeast of Phoenix in Gila and Graham counties. Along with basketry and pottery, the San Carlos Apaches create unusual jewelry set with peridots, pale green semi-precious gemstones found in that area.
San Carlos Apache Tribal Council
P. O. Box O
San Carlos, AZ 85550
(602) 475-2361

Tonto-Apache Reservation, 94 miles northeast of Phoenix in Gila County. Native crafts of basketry and beadwork are emphasized.
Tonto-Apache Tribal Council
P. O. Box 1440
Payson, AZ 85541
(602) 474-5000

Yavapai-Prescott Reservation, 103 miles northwest of Phoenix in Yavapai County. Best bet for collecting native baskets.
Yavapai-Prescott Tribal Council
P. O. Box 348
Prescott, AZ 86302
(602) 445-8790

For more information about Arizona's Indian tribes contact:
Arizona Commission of Indian Affairs
1695 W. Jefferson
Phoenix, AZ 85007
(602) 255-3123

Arizona State Parks

Land of the great outdoors, Arizona has 19 state parks with historical and recreational settings. Each offers strollers, hikers, boaters, backpackers and climbers a variety of experiences. Twelve of the recreational parks have hiking trails, and six of those include equestrian trails. Campground facilities are available at 11 of the parks, and seven offer boating opportunities. There is a nominal per-vehicle fee charged at each park. For more information on any of the state parks, call or write to:

Arizona State Parks
1688 W. Adams St.
Phoenix, AZ 85007
(602) 255-4174

For specific information on Arizona trails and hiking, write for information to:

Arizona State Parks, Trails Coordinator
1688 W. Adams St.
Phoenix, AZ 85007
(602) 255-4174

Flagstaff Parks and Recreation Department
1850 N. Turquoise Dr.
Flagstaff, AZ 86001
(602) 779-4154

THE GREAT OUTDOORS

Regional Information

Arizona is divided into 15 counties; and not all of them have recreation departments. For information concerning local trails and bike paths, contact the Board of Supervisors in the area which interests you. Following is a list of recreation departments for Arizona's three largest metropolitan areas:

Phoenix

Maricopa County Parks and Recreation Department
4701 E. Washington St.
Phoenix, AZ 85034
(602) 262-3711

Phoenix Parks, Recreation and Library Department
125 E. Washington St.
Phoenix, AZ 85004
(602) 262-6861

Tucson

Pima County Parks and Recreation Department
1204 W. Silverlake Rd.
Tucson, AZ 85713
(602) 882-2680

Tucson City Parks and Recreation Department
900 S. Randolph Way
Tucson, AZ 85716
(602) 791-4873

Flagstaff

Coconino County Parks and Recreation Department
Coconino County Courthouse
Flagstaff, AZ 86001
(602) 779-6631

Flagstaff Parks and Recreation Department
1850 N. Turquoise Drive
Flagstaff, AZ 86001
(602) 779-4154

REGIONAL INFORMATION

PHOENIX

NORTH FROM PHOENIX

DAY TRIP 1
Prescott Valley Chamber of Commerce
3403 Cochise Rd.
Prescott Valley, AZ 86312
(602) 772-8857

Yarnell Chamber of Commerce
P. O. Box 275
Yarnell, AZ 85362
(602) 427-6224

DAY TRIP 2
Phoenix and Valley of the Sun Convention and Visitors Bureau
4455 E. Camelback Rd., Suite 146
Phoenix, AZ 85018
(602) 952-8687

Camp Verde Chamber of Commerce
P. O. Box 1665
Camp Verde, AZ 86322
(602) 567-9294

Jerome Chamber of Commerce
P. O. Box 788
Jerome, AZ 86331
(602) 634-5716

DAY TRIP 3
Sedona-Oak Creek Canyon Chamber of Commerce
P.O. Box 478
Sedona, AZ 86336
(602) 282-7722

DAY TRIP 4
Flagstaff Chamber of Commerce
101 West Santa Fe Ave.
Flagstaff, AZ 86001
(602) 774-4505

NORTHEAST FROM PHOENIX

DAY TRIP 1
Carefree Chamber of Commerce and Cave Creek Chamber of Commerce
P. O. Box 734
Carefree, AZ 85377
(602) 488-3381

DAY TRIP 2
Payson Chamber of Commerce
Corner of AZ-87 and Main St.
Payson, AZ 85547
(602) 474-4515

EAST FROM PHOENIX

DAY TRIP 1
Scottsdale Chamber of Commerce
7333 Scottsdale Mall
Scottsdale, AZ 85251
(602) 945-8481

Fountain Hills Chamber of Commerce
12635 North Saguaro Blvd.
Fountain Hills, AZ 85268
(602) 837-1654

DAY TRIP 2
Tempe Chamber of Commerce
504 East Southern Ave.
Tempe, AZ 85282
(602) 967-7891

Mesa Convention and Visitors Bureau
10 West First St.
Mesa, AZ 85201
(602) 969-1307

Apache Junction Chamber of Commerce
1001 North Idaho Rd.
Apache Junction, AZ 85220
(602) 982-3141

DAY TRIP 3
Greater Globe-Miami Chamber of Commerce
1450 North Broad St.
Globe, AZ 85502
(602) 425-4495

Show Low Chamber of Commerce
P. O. Box 1083
Show Low, AZ 85901
(602) 537-2326

SOUTHEAST FROM PHOENIX

DAY TRIP 1
Pinal County Visitors Center
P. O. Box 967
Florence, AZ 85232
(602) 868-4331

Coolidge Chamber of Commerce
320 West Central Ave.
Coolidge, AZ 85228
(602) 723-3009

Casa Grande Chamber of Commerce
575 North Marshall
Casa Grande, AZ 85222
(602) 836-2125

DAY TRIP 2
Metropolitan Tucson Convention and Visitors Bureau
450 West Paseo Redondo
Tucson, AZ 85705
(602) 624-1817

SOUTH FROM PHOENIX

DAY TRIP 1
Casa Grande Chamber of Commerce
575 North Marshall
Casa Grande, AZ 85222
(602) 836-2125

SOUTHWEST FROM PHOENIX

DAY TRIP 1
Gila Bend Chamber of Commerce
P. O. Box CC
Gila Bend, AZ 85337
No Phone

Yuma Civic and Convention Center
1440 Desert Hills Dr.
Yuma, AZ 85364
(602) 344-3800

WEST FROM PHOENIX

DAY TRIP 1
Lake Havasu Area Visitor and Convention Bureau
65 N. Lake Havasu Ave.
Lake Havasu City, AZ 86403
(602) 453-3444

Parker Chamber of Commerce
1217 California Ave.
Parker, AZ 85344
(602) 669-2174

NORTHWEST FROM PHOENIX

DAY TRIP 1
Glendale Chamber of Commerce
7125 North 58th Dr.
Glendale, AZ 85301
(602) 937-4754

Peoria Chamber of Commerce
8322 West Washington
Peoria, AZ 85345
(602) 979-3601

Wickenburg Chamber of Commerce
P. O. Drawer CC
Wickenburg, AZ 85358
(602) 684-5479

TUCSON

NORTHEAST FROM TUCSON

DAY TRIP 1
Metropolitan Tucson Convention and Visitors Bureau
450 West Paseo Redondo
Tucson, AZ 85705
(602) 624-1817

EAST FROM TUCSON

DAY TRIP 1
Metropolitan Tucson Convention and Visitors Bureau
450 West Paseo Redondo
Tucson, AZ 85705
(602) 624-1817

DAY TRIP 2
Benson Chamber of Commerce
P. O. Box 2255
Benson, AZ 85602
(602) 586-2842

Willcox Chamber of Commerce
1500 North Circle I Rd.
Willcox, AZ 85643
(602) 384-2272

Safford-Graham County Chamber of Commerce
1111 Thatcher Blvd.
Safford, AZ 85546
(602) 428-2511

DAY TRIP 3
Willcox Chamber of Commerce
1500 North Circle I Rd.
Willcox, AZ 85643
(602) 384-2272

SOUTHEAST OF TUCSON

DAY TRIP 1
Tombstone Tourism Association
P. O. Box 917
Tombstone, AZ 85638
(602) 457-2211

Bisbee Chamber of Commerce
78 Main St.
Bisbee, AZ 85603
(602) 432-2141

Sierra Vista Chamber of Commerce
416 Sherbundy
Sierra Vista, AZ 85635
(602) 458-6940

SOUTH FROM TUCSON

DAY TRIP 1
Nogales-Santa Cruz County Chamber of Commerce
Kino Park
Nogales, AZ 85621
(602) 287-3685

DAY TRIP 2
Metropolitan Tucson Convention and Visitors Bureau
450 West Paseo Redondo
Tucson, AZ 85705
(602) 624-1817

SOUTHWEST OF TUCSON

DAY TRIP 1
Metropolitan Tucson Convention and Visitors Bureau
450 West Paseo Redondo
Tucson, AZ 85705
(602) 624-1817

WEST OF TUCSON

DAY TRIP 1
Metropolitan Tucson Convention and Visitors Bureau
450 West Paseo Redondo
Tucson, AZ 85705
(602) 624-1817

NORTHWEST FROM TUCSON

DAY TRIP 1
Phoenix and Valley of The Sun Convention and Visitors Bureau
4455 E. Camelback Rd., Suite 146
Phoenix, AZ 85018
(602) 952-8687

FLAGSTAFF

NORTH FROM FLAGSTAFF

DAY TRIP 1
Flagstaff Chamber of Commerce
101 West Santa Fe Ave.
Flagstaff, AZ 86001
(602) 774-4505

Page/Lake Powell Chamber of Commerce
6 Lake Powell Blvd.
Page, AZ 86040
(602) 645-2741

NORTHEAST FROM FLAGSTAFF

DAY TRIP 1
Navajo Reservation
Cultural Resources Department
Visitors Services
P. O. Box 308
Window Rock, AZ 86515
(602) 871-4941
(Note that Window Rock is the headquarters for the Navajo nation.)

DAY TRIP 2
Canyon de Chelly National Monument
Box 588
Chinle, AZ 86503
(602) 674-5436

DAY TRIP 3
Hopi Tribal Council
P. O. Box 123
Kyakotsmovi, AZ 86039
(602) 734-2445

EAST FROM FLAGSTAFF

DAY TRIP 1
Holbrook-Petrified Forest Chamber of Commerce
325 Navajo Blvd.
Holbrook, AZ 86025
(602) 524-6558

SOUTHEAST FROM FLAGSTAFF

DAY TRIP 1
Flagstaff Chamber of Commerce
101 West Santa Fe Ave.
Flagstaff, AZ 86001
(602) 774-4505

Payson Chamber of Commerce
Corner of A-87 and Main Street
Payson, AZ 85547
(602) 474-4515

SOUTH FROM FLAGSTAFF

DAY TRIP 1
Sedona-Oak Creek Canyon Chamber of Commerce
P. O. Box 478
Sedona, AZ 86336
(602) 282-7722

SOUTHWEST FROM FLAGSTAFF

DAY TRIP 1
Jerome Chamber of Commerce
P. O. Box 788
Jerome, AZ 86331
(602) 634-5716

Prescott Chamber of Commerce
117 West Goodwin St.
Prescott, AZ 85935
(602) 445-2000

WEST FROM FLAGSTAFF

DAY TRIP 1
Williams/Grand Canyon Chamber of Commerce
820 West Bill Williams Ave.
Williams, AZ 86046
(602) 635-2041

NORTH FROM FLAGSTAFF

DAY TRIP 1
Grand Canyon National Park
Back Country Reservation Office
P. O. Box 129
Grand Canyon, AZ 86023
(602) 638-2474

Grand Canyon National Park Lodges
Reservation Department
P. O. Box 699
Grand Canyon, AZ 86023
(602) 638-2631

Tourist Safety Tips

The following information is reprinted from *The 1984 KOY Almanac* edited by Pam Hait with permission. ©1984 by Gary Edens.

FLASH FLOODS

When a violent thunderstorm breaks over the mountains and deserts of the Southwest, runoff from the torrential rains cascades into the steep canyons in a matter of minutes. Walls of water, sometimes 10 to 30 feet high, swirl through the canyons and arroyos picking up mud, boulders, trees and other debris. Plants, animals and sometimes man are caught and swept along for a flash flood stops at nothing which is unlucky enough to be in its path.

Flash floods can result from thunderstorms miles away and can occur in Arizona at any time of the year. However, the predominant seasons are summer and early fall. Isolated thunderstorms are the main cause from late June through mid-September, while tropical storms or Pacific storms are the main culprit from August through October.

A thunderstorm cloud called a cumulonimbus is a large, towering formation which frequently spreads out at the top into the shape of an anvil. This cloud usually appears dark and threatening when viewed from below, but very bright and white when seen from the side at some distance.

The National Weather Service issues a Flash Flood Watch when such a flood is a possibility. A Flash Flood Warning is issued when flash flooding has been reported or radar indicates heavy rain in a flood-prone area.

WHAT TO DO

1. Stay tuned to a radio station which gives flood watch warnings.
2. Keep an eye on the sky and watch for thunderstorms.
3. Avoid deep canyons and dry washes during stormy or threatening weather.
4. Camp on high ground but not on top of exposed peaks or ridges.
5. Never cross a flooded dip in the roadway. The water may be deeper than you think or the roadway washed away.
6. If your vehicle is stuck in a low-lying area, abandon it and move to higher ground.

6. If your vehicle is stuck in a low-lying area, abandon it and move to higher ground.
7. If local authorities want you to leave an area — leave. People die needlessly because they ignore warnings to seek safety.
8. Inform someone of your destination and when you expect to return. Police should be notified immediately if you do not return on time.

DESERT SURVIVAL

Having great weather year-round means that Arizonans spend more time outdoors than most people in the country. With the elegant Sonoran desert surrounding us, it's no wonder that the urge is to get out and enjoy it. Unfortunately, too many people go out into the desert unprepared. Here are some important desert survival tips to remember.

THREE RULES OF DESERT SURVIVAL

Never Alone

Tell Someone

Stay Put

If you do get lost, make a large X — at least 14 feet long — where you are. This can be made by dragging your foot, breaking off bush branches, or any other means at your disposal.

Start blowing a whistle at regular intervals using three short blasts. This is the international distress signal.

Light three fires in the shape of a triangle near where you are. This is a good signal both day and night.

Don't eat in the desert. Eating draws fluid out of your body and makes you dehydrate faster.

Keep a water jug with a straw in the car. Remember that children dehydrate quicker than adults.

Remember these three points about water in the desert: *TAKE IT, DRINK IT,* and *DON'T SAVE IT!*

Finally, always tell someone the make of your car, its color, where you are going and when you'll be back. This will make it easier for searchers to find you.

THE CLIMATE
OF ARIZONA

Arizona is a land of dramatic contrasts, as varied in its climate as in its beauty. Temperatures and rainfall vary tremendously throughout the three main topographical areas within the state, for extremes in elevation are matched by extremes in temperatures. These three topographical areas can roughly be divided as follows:

The high plateau — elevations average 5000 to 7000 feet.

The desert mountain and valleys.

The mountains — with peaks from 9000 to 12,000 feet.

Temperatures can range as much as 60 degrees in a single day due to the dry air normally over the state, but generally average temperatures are governed by elevation. As a rule of thumb, figure on a 3½° F. difference for every 1000-foot change in altitude.

When it comes to extremes, there are usually worse days on record! The hottest daytime temperature ever recorded was 127° F. at Parker in 1905. The coldest day on record was minus 40° F. at Hawley Lake on January 7, 1971. Of course new records are always being set. Both July 14, 1982, with 113° F. recorded, and September 6, 1982, with 110° F., set new high maximum temperatures for those dates. From the beginning to the end of October, the greatest temperature changes are recorded in Phoenix — greater changes than any seen during the year in Central Arizona. By November, the mild winter season is established in the Salt River Valley.

Sunshine in Phoenix averages 86 percent of the possible amount, ranging from a minimum monthly average of about 77 percent in January and December to a maximum of about 94 percent in June.

Elevation and season also affect the amount of rain and snow that Arizona receives. These amounts vary dramatically. On the average, some desert areas only have three to four inches of rain a year, while certain mountain areas received up to 30 inches. Pacific storms cause most of the rainfall from November through March with winter snowfall totals sometimes reaching 100 inches on the highest mountains. Summer rainfall begins in July and extends through mid-September when moisture-bearing winds from the southeast and south cause the Arizona monsoon. The thunderstorms which result can cause strong winds, blinding dust storms and local heavy rainfall. Heavy thunderstorms can cause flash flooding and while major flooding is rare, it can — and does — happen.

Dry spells can last for many months but count on April through June as the driest part of the year anywhere in the state. However, when thunderstorms occur, they can be wild. The damaging winds accompanying these storms are usually straight-line winds which can move in at speeds upwards of 75 miles per hour.

HEAT WAVE SAFETY RULES

If you are not used to the extreme heat that can occur in the desert, it's easy to over do it and even get sick. Below are some basic rules for living in — and even enjoying — Arizona's high temperature times.

1. **Slow Down.** Your body cannot keep up with extremely high temperatures, expecially when the humidity rises.
2. **Dress For Summer.** Lightweight, light-colored clothing reflects the heat and sunlight and helps maintain normal body temperatures.
3. **Put Less Fuel In Your Inner Fires.** Foods like proteins that increase metabolic heat production also increase water loss.
4. **Don't Dry Out.** Hot weather can wring the water out of you before you know it's happened. The first sign of dehydration is being cross. Recognize this symptom and drink lots of water when the weather is hot.
5. **Don't Get Too Much Sun.** Sunburn makes the job of heat dissipation that much more difficult. Not only is sunburn uncomfortable, but too much sun invites skin cancer. Wear a good, protective sunscreen whenever you are in the sun.
6. **Take Care Of The Children and Pets.** Never leave the kids or animals in the car on a hot day — not even for that quick trip into a store.
7. **Vary Your Thermal Environment.** Try to get out of the heat for at least a few hours each day.

Enjoy other quality guides from Globe Pequot Press featuring the Southwest:

Day Trips from Houston
Guide to the Recommended Country Inns of Arizona,
New Mexico, and Texas
Journey to the High Southwest
Photographing the North American West

Available at your bookstore or direct from the publisher. For a free catalogue or to place an order, call 1-800-243-0495 (in Connecticut, call 1-800-962-0973) or write to The Globe Pequot Press, 138 West Main Street, Chester, Connecticut 06412.